The Underground Railroad
and
The Picayune Connection

Harry F. Dill

HERITAGE BOOKS
2012

HERITAGE BOOKS
AN IMPRINT OF HERITAGE BOOKS, INC.

Books, CDs, and more—Worldwide

For our listing of thousands of titles see our website at
www.HeritageBooks.com

Published 2012 by
HERITAGE BOOKS, INC.
Publishing Division
100 Railroad Ave. #104
Westminster, Maryland 21157

Copyright © 1998 Harry F. Dill

Other Heritage Books by the author:

African American Inhabitants of Rapides Parish, Louisiana: 15 June–4 September 1870

Appointments of Postmasters in Louisiana, 12 January 1827–28 December 1892

Louisiana Postmistress and Postmaster Appointments 20 June 1866–17 November 1931

Marriages and Deaths from The Caucasian, *Shreveport, Louisiana, 1903–1913*

Some Slaveholders and Their Slaves, Union Parish, Louisiana, 1839–1865
Harry F. Dill and William Simpson

The Underground Railroad and the Picayune *Connection*

All rights reserved. No part of this book may be reproduced or transmitted in any form or by any means, electronic or mechanical, including photocopying, recording or by any information storage and retrieval system without written permission from the author, except for the inclusion of brief quotations in a review.

International Standard Book Numbers
Paperbound: 978-0-7884-1057-4
Clothbound: 978-0-7884-9443-7

Table of Contents

Preface v
The Connection Begins 1
Index, Slaveholders and Others 129
Index, Slaves, Full Names 143
Index, Slaves, First Names Only 147

Preface

On 27 January 1837, The Picayune, a 6-page daily newspaper was established in New Orleans, Louisiana. Its name was changed to The Daily Picayune on 2 November 1837, but layout and content remained essentially the same as those of its predecessor.

Local and out-of-state news, editorials, essays, poetry, human interest stories, reports of arrivals and departures of vessels and steamboats, and advertisements (many offering rewards for runaway slaves) filled the pages of The Picayune and The Daily Picayune.

Microfilm of the papers, on file at Louisiana State University at Alexandria, Louisiana, a satellite college of LSU at Baton Rouge, can provide for many readers, fascinating glimpses of the people who lived during the period covered by this book (27 Jan 1837--26 Dec 1847), their customs, institutions, mores, and creature comforts.

For persons seeking slave ancestors, the ads are valuable resources. Names of slaves, usually first names only, but quite often full names as well; brief but vivid descriptions of slaves; dates they ran away; their trades or occupations; names of owners or persons holding them in custody, and other details, present a trove for slave descendants.

Although some ads lack names of slaveholders, I have included names of slaves and other clues that could lead to discovery of slave ancestors. Non-essential items have been eliminated, such as, clothing worn, and street addresses of owners.

The first ad offering a reward for a slave named Hannah, appeared in the 16 March 1837 issue of The Picayune (see p. 1).

The Connection Begins

HORSES AND NEGRO LOST.

Strayed from 92 Custom House Street, early in December last, two Mares, one a brown, with long mane and tail, about 14 hands high, more than 12 years old; the other a blood bay, with short nicked tail, near 15 hands high, 4 years old; both remarkably gay, and fast trotters, with no white marks upon either.

Also, late in December, a tall slender Negro woman, named HANNAH, about 40 years of age, with but one eye. One half the value of the negro will be given to any person who will return the horses; or one-half the negro will be given to the Orphan Asylum, upon her being reclaimed for the owner.

The Lafayette Gazette will publish the above 4 weeks, and send the account to 92 for payment.

FIVE DOLLARS REWARD.

Ranaway from the subscriber, about the 15th March last, a negro woman called CELIA belonging to S. D. Dixon, aged 45; she is a dark griffe, a little lame in one hip. Apply to 16, Camp st.

$500 REWARD.

Ranaway from the subscriber, on Saturday the 18th of March last, a negro girl named MARIAH, aged from 28 to 30 years, about 5 feet 4 or 5 inches in height, heavy made, a dark griffe, large mouth, and in the habit of laughing when spoken to. She speaks French a little, and is slightly pitted with the small pox. She will probably try to pass herself off as a hair dresser, or as a boy, as she has frequently dressed herself in boy's clothes, and has her hair cut short for the purpose. She will doubtless deny to whom she belongs. The above reward will be paid for information and sufficient evidence to convict the person who is now harboring said Mariah. Twenty dollars will be paid for her if in any jail in this state, or ten dollars out of it. Apply to

H. F. WADE,
No. 55 Tchapitoulas street.

9 Apr 1837. $10 Reward. Ran away on the 4th instant, my black girl ROSA or DIDO, aged about 11, 4' 10", thick set, full face--has a mark on one of her arms, one on the neck, and another on one of her feet, occasioned by a scald or burn. She has been but a short while in the city. E. B. KELLY.

9 Apr 1837. $10 Reward. Ran away from me at Fauxbourg, Marigay, on the 8th, a mulatto man by name of MACE, sometimes calls himself DORSEY, about 40 or 45, about 6', thin, spare made, with broad whiskers. JAMES GARRET.

28 Apr 1837. $20 Reward. Ran away on the 18th of March a negro girl named MARIAH, aged from 28 to 30, about 5' 5", heavy made, a dark griffe, large mouth, speaks French a little. She is slightly pitted with smallpox. She may try to pass herself off as a hair dresser, or as a boy, as she has frequently dressed in boy's clothes and has her hair cut short for that purpose. H. F. WADE.

7 May 1837.   Caution to Shipmasters and Masters
                           of Steamboats
My slave, CAROLINE, of a dark mulatto complexion, aged about 30, 5' 3", absconded from my house on the 26th of April and has since been seen on the Levee in man's clothes--it is supposed she will attempt to leave the city aboard a seagoing vessel. JAMES M. TAYLOR.

25 Jun 1837. $20 Reward. Will be paid for apprehension of the boy LEROY--12 years old, slender built, high cheek bones and sharp chin. Leroy ran away from my plantation at Manchac February or March last. ABRAHAM MCGEHEE.

3 Jul 1837. Ran away about the 1st of May a negro man named ISAAC BENNETT, about 28, 5' 8 or 9", black. He belongs to Capt. C. S. Longcope, of Belle Isle, Miss. A

reasonable reward will be paid when delivered to IRWIN, HALL & WALTON.

5 Jul 1837. $20 Reward. Ran away about the last of June, a negro boy named REASON, 18, thin featured, high cheek bones, very white teeth, long flat feet and stoops when walking. GEORGE S. JOHNSTON.

10 Jul 1837. $20 Reward. Ran away while on trial at the house of Madam Pucheu, on the 7th instant, a bright mulatto man named WILLIAM, 22, about 5' 8", very likely, intelligent, sprightly, active and quick spoken. S. BENNETT.

11 Sep 1837. $20 Reward. Will be paid for apprehension of the negro man GEORGE, who absconded on the 2d inst. He is about 6' 2", well proportioned; looks down when spoken to. He is aged about 22.

13 Sep 1837. $20 Reward. For the negro boys, WORNER and JACKSON. Worner is about 22, about 5' 8". He is quick spoken, has an impediment in his speech and is ruptured. Jackson is about 30, about 5' 6". JONES & TURNER.

27 Sep 1837. $5 Reward. Ran away on the 25th of September, the negro woman, SABRINA, with her boy, 3 years old. She was bought from Mr. Randolph about 4 months ago. She is black, with high cheek bones. She is very lusty and walks pigeon-toed. L. JONES.

6 Jan 1838. Ran away on Sunday last a negro woman ELIZA, about 35, and left at my residence 2 children. JAMES H. SYLVESTER.

6 Mar 1838. $10 Reward. Absconded from Fauxbourg St. Mary, 3 weeks ago, a mulatto man DICK. Has a pleasant countenance and smiles when spoken to. SLOANE & CO.

3 Apr 1838. $50 Reward. Ran away on the 21st of Feb. near Rodney, Miss., a slave boy by the name of HENRY, 24 or 25, about 5' 10". WILLIAM H. COMPTON.

4 Apr 1838. $50 Reward. Strayed or stolen on the 28th ultimo a black boy aged 12 years named JACK. P. M. TOURNE.

9 Jun 1838. $100 Reward. Ran away the 2d instant, a negro boy named TURNER, about 18, 5' 7", slim stature, small eyes, lank cheeks. He is accustomed to wait about the house, is artful, can cook. JAMES EVANS.

22 Jun 1838. $100 Reward. Ran away from Franklin Hall the 17th inst. the slave PETER, about 12 or 13, very black, high forehead, small hands and feet. L. A. CALDWELL.

8 Jul 1838.   A Runaway in Jail
Committed to jail in New Orleans on the 25th ult. a stout negro boy, perfectly black, who calls himself JIM, about 21, and says he was originally brought from Virginia, but lately from Alabama--that he was bought by a man near the Lower Market named Le Roude (or something like it) for a negro woman (French) who lives down the coast. Owner is requested to prove property, pay charges, and take him away. Said slave was found on board the steamer Tiber. STEPHEN JOHNSON, Captain of the Tiber.

11 Jul 1838. $100 Reward. Absconded about 3 months ago, the negro boy GEORGE, about 18 or 20, flat nose and thick

lips, speaks French and English. Is supposed to have gone away with a mulatto man named John, who calls himself free.

15 Jul 1838. $75 Reward. Ran away on the 11th of July, the slaves: GEORGE, about 35, 5' 10", jet black, a bricklayer by trade, rather stout; VIOLET, jet black, about 25, speaks French and English, front teeth bad; MARY ANN, jet black, rough skin, about 16, about 5' 4" tall. They were recently purchased in Mobile. SHERMAN JOHNSON.

29 Jul 1838. $50 reward will be paid for apprehending the slave JOHN, who absconded from my yard on the 11th of June. He is about 4' 5", 12 to 14 years old, very black and stout. Speaks only English.

9 Aug 1838. $20 Reward will be paid for delivery of the boy NATHAN, a dark mulatto, 16 or 17, recently from Vicksburg. His hair is cut very close with a hand saw across the back. GEORGE A. BOTTS.

9 Aug 1838. $20 reward for NAN or NANNAH, a very black negress, about 24, a creole, speaks French and English. She formerly belonged to Mr. Sarpe in the 3d Municipality. GEORGE A. BOTTS.

18 Aug 1838. $20 Reward. Will be paid for arrest of the boy ANDREW, who absconded on the 5th inst. He is about 15, 5' tall, black, stammers a little. JOHN MINTURN.

21 Aug 1838. $20 reward will be paid for apprehension of the bright mulattress ELIZABETH, who ran away Sunday evening last. She belongs to the succession of Elihu Shuids. JAMES M. TAYLOR.

2 Aug 1838. $20 Reward. Ran away the 23d ultimo NED, a negro slave about 22, 5' 9", very black, compactly built, has a scar over one eye; speaks English, French and Spanish. He was raised in New Orleans and has been a drummer. ISAAC LAZARUS, Covington, La.

5 Aug 1838. $5 Reward. Ran away on the 28th of July the negro woman HARRIET TOUSAINT, formerly belonging to the estate of TOUSAINT GUIYOM, butcher in the city, sold by the court of probates about 10 days ago. She is of middle size, not very black, speaks English, French and Spanish. LAWRENCE JONES.

26 Aug 1838. $25 Reward. Will be given for the negro GEORGE belonging to Mrs. Carter of Woodville, Miss., who absconded about the 18th inst. He is about 6' tall, stout, black complexion, 2 upper teeth broken.

20 Sep 1838. $25 reward for apprehension the negro woman JENNY, who ran away the 17th, with her 2 children, one 10 years old, the other about 11 months. She is 5' tall, 34, marked by the smallpox. She speaks French and English. P. RIVIERE.

2 Oct 1838. $15 Reward. Ran away 23 Sep. a griffe boy named WASHINGTON, about 21, 5' 6" high.

2 Oct 1838. $25 reward. Absconded 23 August a negro woman named AGGY, about 35, slim made, no upper front teeth, speaks English only. M. Robetaile.

7 Oct 1838. $10 Reward. Ran away a griff man named JOHN BELL, aged 30, stout built, 5' 11", has a scar on his left cheek; speaks English and some French. GEORGE MERRICK.

6

31 Oct 1838. $10 Reward. Ran away yesterday the slave CATHERINE, a griffe, aged about 30, speaks French and English. DOYLE & MAY.

1 Nov 1838. $50 reward. Ran away last month from my plantation in Amite Co., Miss., ABERDEEN and STEPHEN. Aberdeen is black, slim made, 28 years old, 5' 11. Stephen is a mulatto, 21, and grum and silent. They were purchased in June from Mr. P. Johnston of Mobile. MATHEW RAMSEY.

7 Nov 1838. $25 Reward. Ran away the 30th ultimo the slave MARIA, a mulatto about 23, 5' high, and very likely. She was sold to me by the Syndic of E. B. Cogswell. She may be under the influence of said Cogswell, as she was once before, while a runaway, and belonging to Mr. John Leslie, harbored by the said Cogswell, who had her concealed in his armoir when found. As further reason for suspicion the said Cogswell had the audacity to call on me and tell me if I kept her she would do me no good, and immediately after disappeared. JOHN R. UNRUH.

20 Nov 1838. $10 Reward. Ran away from the subscriber the negro boy BOB, about 5' 10", well built, speaks French and English. He formerly belonged to Mr. Welsh's saw mill. He is about 27. CHARLES MEYER.

8 Dec 1838. $15 Reward. For the girl CLARISSA, small size, copper complexion, about 28, 2 or 3 upper teeth missing, a small piece out of her upper right ear. ISHAM GRIFFIN.

27 Dec 1838. $10 Reward. Ran away the slave LOUISE, a stout fleshy griffe colored woman about 5' tall, speaks French, English and Spanish. J. HALL.

9 Jan 1839. $50 Reward. Ran away on Wednesday a yellow boy named JOHN, about 35, 5' 7 or 8", with large whiskers and several teeth out in front. Was engaged previous to running away in cooking for Mr. Brady in Charles st. He was formerly the property of Thomas Suggit.

8 Jan 1839. $10 Reward. Ran away from me the negress NANCY, stout built, about 24, tongue-tied. FRANCIS MAGUIRE.

24 Jan 1839. $20 Reward. Ran away the 20th inst. from the plantation of R. A. Wilkinson, below the city, the negro boy COLBERT, a bright mulatto, 5' 9 or 10", 23 years old.

2 Mar 1839. $50 Reward. Ran away from the Mississippi Cotton Press, WASHINGTON and SAM. Washington is about 28, 5' 7", has a mark on one shoulder caused by a cut. Sam is 20, 5' 10 or 11", with a scar on his forehead. Both boys are black. H. V. BAXTER.

13 Mar 1839. $20 Reward. Ran away the 28th of Feb., JAMES RICHARDSON, a negro 25 years old, 5' 6", his face marked by smallpox; has lost 3 of his upper front teeth.

23 Mar 1838. $200 Reward. For apprehension of a mulatto woman named CATHERINE, small stature, about 30, straight hair, rings on her fingers. She was raised by Judge White of Tennessee, and is quite intelligent. It is probable she has gone to Vicksburg as she was formerly owned there and has a husband there. S. H. COULTER.

31 Mar 1839. $10 Reward. For arrest of the negress SIDNEY or LOUCINDA, about 35, 5' 4", somewhat fat, and marked with the smallpox. She absconded from my plantation 2 weeks since. She has some free relations in the city. J. DAVIS, Jr.

2 Apr 1839. $50 Reward. Ran away last month a dark mulatto named WILLIAM, about 22, kinky hair, 5' 6", understands both shaving and cooking; sometimes wears earrings for which his ears are bored. He was formerly owned by Madam Lynn. JOHN C. BEASLY, Plaquemine.

7 Apr 1839. $25 Reward. Ran away the 25th of March a mulatto boy named TOM, 5' 9 or 10", 22. Is a carriage driver. He was purchased in December from a Mr. Slatter who brought him here from Virginia. JAMES B. DIGGS.

7 Apr 1839. $25 Reward. Ran away last evening the slave girl MARY JANE, about 20, remarkably white for a slave. WILLIAM COLLERTON.

7 Apr 1839. $10 Reward. JOHN SOLET, a young mulatto about 20, 5' 10", a cooper by trade, ran away from my plantation on Saturday. He may try to pass himself off as a free man, under the name of John Mitchell, alias John Wilson. JOSEPH B. WILKINSON.

12 Apr 1839. Dr. Dalton will pay $20 for delivery of his negro boy JACK. He is about 17 years old, very smart and intelligent, speaks French and English, and, I am told, is now studying Spanish.

18 Apr 1839. $25 Reward. For my slave WILLIAM or BILL, a cook by trade; he is about 5' 8", 25, a little stoop-shouldered. He has a wife somewhere in Esplanade st. He had a chain to his leg when he left the City Hotel. GEORGE P. SHALL.

29 Sep 1839. $100 Reward will be paid for apprehension of the slave FRENCH, who disappeared the 8th of August. He is about 5' 8".

20 Apr 1839. $50 Reward. Ran away or stolen Sunday night the negro TOM SHIRLEY. He is of black complexion, slender made, about 16 years old. A. H. WALLACE & CO.

1 May 1839. $50 Reward. Ran away from my plantation in Wilkinson Co., Miss., near Cold Springs Post Office, a negro named PATRICK, about 30, 6 feet high, very black. He can do very good work with tools. He dresses fine and has a fine stock of clothes and some gold rings. He drove a dray for 3 years in Natchez. THOMAS J. LANIER.

11 May 1839. Ran away from me Thursday last the mulatto girl SUSAN, about 18, straight hair, small scar under her left eye, slender built. MARTHA GRAY.

16 May 1839. Whereas a certain HAMBRIGHT BLACK did on the 17th April last take from Rosne Co., Tenn., 14 negroes, which by the judgment of the Supreme Court of said State, he was enjoined from taking away--said negroes by judgment of said court being entitled to their freedom, and a bill now pending in Chancery Court for their emancipation. The negroes consist of a man named GEORGE, quite black, his wife SIDNEY, AMY a sister of SIDNEY, both likely women. The balance are children, to wit, EDMOND, RUFUS, CALVIZ, LORENZO, NEWTON, ANDERSON, very white, and one girl ELLEN, other names not recollected. L. W. JORDAN, Kingston, Tenn.

16 May 1839. $50 Reward. Will be paid for apprehension of the boy FIELD, quite black, 5' 4", aged 25, speaks French and English fluently. He left the 13th inst. D'AQUIN BROTHERS.

16 May 1839. $30 Reward. Ran away the 30th of April, the girl FRANCES, about 16, black, very intelligent, her ears pierced for rings. GEORGE P. SHALL.

1 June 1839. $25 Reward. Ran away or stolen on 22d May a black fellow named JANUARY, about 5' 8", 22, has a scar on his forehead and one near his left eye; stutters when talking. He has a wife in Vicksburg and may try to go there. H. F. WADE.

2 Jun 1839. $200 Reward. Ran away in May from on board the steamer Meridian, lying at the Lake end of the Ponchartrain railroad, 2 negro men: PRIMUS, about 5' 8", 35, black complexion, speaks well, reads and writes and plays on the violin. One of his hands has been burnt leaving a light scar. Also CAESAR, about 5' 11", 25, also reads and writes and plays on the violin. BOYKIN & NORISS, Mobile.

4 Jun 1839. $50 Reward. Ran away on 29th April my black girl FRANCES, 15 or 16 years old, small size. She has absconded several times before, and been in the habit of changing her name: the last time she passed as Mary Ann Jones. Her ears are bored for rings. WILLIAM H. AVERY.

7 Jun 1839. $50 Reward. Ran away on 23 April my mulatto boy CHARLES--he is apparently 16, but in fact 19 or 20, rather small, about 5' 3", of a bright mulatto complexion with straight black hair. He is an excellent body and house servant. He often tries to conceal with false hair a large bald spot on his head. THOMAS ARMAT, Nachez, Miss.

7 Jun 1839. $100 Reward! Ran away from the subscriber's plantation near Bayou Sara, on 23 May, a negro named WILLIAM, about 20, 5' 2", stout made, has a large scar on his left hand, caused by a burn, also one above the left eye. When

stripped, many scars can be seen on his back, caused from a severe whipping with a cowskin (he says) at the time of the Southampton insurrection. He was purchased in Vicksburg by Mr. S. N. Hite and last winter by me from Mr. Hite. He ran away in April, was caught and put in jail in Woodville, Miss. W. J. FROST, Woodville, Miss.

13 Jun 1839. $50 Reward. Ran away on the 1st inst. a black boy, about 30, 5' 6", named RALPH, very black, has a scar on one of his legs caused by a dray, well known in this city as a drayman. WILLIAM BARKLEY.

18 Jun 1839. $100 Reward will be given for arrest of a copper colored negro man named DENNIS, who ran away from Daniel D. Page of St. Louis on the 5th inst. He is about 5' 4", is a baker by trade and well known in St. Louis and Louisville as a carrier of bread on board steamboats for Daniel D. Page, who purchased him from Capt. Shroder in Louisville. DOUGHERTY & CO.

19 Jun 1839. Stolen at Monticello, Florida, May 25th, a negro named GEORGE, belonging to John C. Neal, and the following negroes: LETTUS, a very black woman, about 46, her son ADAM, about 9; SUSAN, her daughter, about 19; and Susan's child, a boy about 1 year old; BENY, a son of Lettus, about 12, and LIZ, a girl about 12. GEORGE is about 5' 6", and is the father of Lettus' children. He always had charge of his master's affairs, can read well. $25 reward will be paid for each one, or $100 for George.

3 Jul 1839. $50 Reward. Will be paid for apprehension of a girl named EVELINA, aged 25, and child, JAMES, about 3 years old. Evelina is a light mulatto, grey eyes, some freckles on her face. She is about 5' 4" and dresses genteel. The child is of a griff color. CHARLES R. GLYNN.

7 Jul 1839. $10 Reward. Ran away from me the 4th inst. a negro woman named SUSAN or SUKEY, aged 25, stout built, her left foot very crooked. She was pruchased of Mr. Moulle on Royal st. about the 1st of April. NATHAN NICHOLS.

13 Jul 1838. $10 Reward. Ran away the 1st inst. the negro boy NELSON, 24 years old, stout make, black complexion, about 5' 9"--belongs to Capt. Harris of Columbus, Ga.

13 Jul 1839. $20 Reward will be given for lodgement in jail of the mulatto boy SAM, about 20. He has a scar between the eyebrows. He is about 5' 8" tall. He was brought here from Helena on the 3d inst. but was raised in the city. He has a brother named Jack Pierre who sells poultry in the 1st municipality. L. D. HYDE.

13 Jul 1839. $150 reward will be paid for my 2 negroes, NED and SOLOMON who ran away last November. Ned is of black color, short stature, and bow-legged, very much marked on the body with smallpox, as he says, but may have been caused by punishment. Ned also ran away from my plantation in June or July 1838. He was purchased of George A. Botts. SOLOMON, black, about 5' 11, Roman nose, one or two spots on his belly caused by burns. Formerly belonged to Edward Folse. BENJAMIN CROSS, Thibodeaux, La.

20 Jul 1839. $50 Reward. Ran away from the Louisiana Bakery on the 18th of May, a negro man generally known as JIM PRICE, about 35, 6' tall, and quite black. For many years he belonged to Mr. Prauche of this city and worked as a butcher. He speaks French and English and is very intelligent. JOHN COTTLE.

21 Jul 1839. $10 Reward. Ran away on the 2d July the boy HERBERT TRIPPLET, aged about 17, 5' high, griff color. PHILIP HARTY, Lafayette, La.

2 Aug 1838. $25 Reward will be paid for arrest of the negress MARY ANN, who ran away yesterday. She was formerly the property of William Porter. She is about 4' 5", and speaks French and English.

3 Aug 1839. $25 Reward will be paid for apprehension of the griffe woman ARY, about 5' 5", who ran away from Carrollton yesterday morning on the 4 o'clock cars. She is very likely, about 25, speaks a little French. She was in the habit of washing in the city 3 years ago.

4 Aug 1839. $50 Reward will be given for the negro man called DAVE, who ran away from Norton's sawmill in Lafayette 4 months ago. He is about 27, 6' high, very black. L. A. CALDWELL.

11 Aug 1839. $150 Reward. Absconded from the steamer Balize on the 7th inst. 3 slaves: NED, thick set, about 25, with a scar on the left side of his forehead, about 5' 7, the property of W. B. G. Taylor. JIM, very black, very tall, and ANDERSON a griff colored negro, very much pockmarked, about 24. The last two belonged to the estate of James Dixon. T. M. WADSWORTH.

13 Aug 1839. $20 Reward. Ran away from the farm of William M. Whitehead, near Livingston Co., Miss., 2 negro men, SAMPSON and HENRY. Sampson is black, with a large Roman nose, a bald head, speaks French tolerably well, is about 45. He left on the 3d June 1838. Henry is of yellow complexion, about 30, 5' 7", one ear bitten or cut off. Is good with carpenter's tools. He left September, 1838.

21 Aug 1839. $25 Reward. Absconded on the 2d inst. a bright mulatto boy named ROBERT, about 25 or 30, about 5' 8", and is knock-kneed. He was purchased from Samuel Locke some months ago, who owned him for the last 4 years. GEORGE P. SHALL.

5 Sep 1839. $20 Reward. Ran away the 20th, my boy BILL, about 5' 6", yellow complexion. He is about 21 and walks a little parrot-toed. He was lately employed at the St. Charles hotel as a waiter. BENJAMIN KENDIG.

3 Oct 1839. $5 Reward. Ran away from Mr. Chandler in Magazine st. on the 1st inst. a creole negress named CHARLOTTE, about 27. She formerly belonged to Adelle Dubuys, and more recently to the Percy family.

6 Oct 1839. $20 Reward. Absconded on the 23d Sep. a negress named JANE, about 30, quite tall; her occupation that of washer and ironer, having little knowledge of other duties of a servant. PETER CONREY.

20 Oct 1839. $20 Reward. Ran away from me on 5th, inst. a dark, freckled negro man named THOMAS TAYLOR, about 5' 10", aged 27, and very badly ruptured (he has on one of Dr. Warner's patent trusses). He was purchased last April from Mr. Dickey of Natchez, Miss., and his wife lives in that city. In May last he was taken up in Natchez and in August last was taken up in New Orleans. THOMAS B. WINSTON.

20 Oct 1839. $10 Reward. Ran away from the subscriber residing in Carrollton on the 28th Sep., a negro girl named SARAH, about 22, brown complexion, full breast, well formed and good looking. Has a scar on one of her feet caused by a burn. FELIX HAYDEN.

26 Oct 1839. $25 Reward. Ran away from me the 22 inst. the negro slave JOHN. He is about 30, stands 5' 10', and very black. He had been here but a few days, having been brought here from New Madrid as a hand on a flatboat. JOHN U. GREEN, Lafayette.

30 Oct 1839. $20 Reward. Ran away from me on the 16th, my black boy ISAAC, upwards of 6 feet. He is an active negro and can turn his hand to almost anything. JOHN TRIMMELL (Milk Man), Parish of Jefferson.

31 Oct 1839. $50 Reward. Ran away a negro named BURREL, about 6', aged 22. Speaks the Indian and French languages. He was raised near Pontotoc, Miss., by a Miss Vicy Colbert. He was recently from Towson, Ark. GEORGE A. BOTTS.

28 Nov 1839. Were brought to the 2d Municipality police prison the following slaves. A negro man named AARON, about 24; says he belongs to John Buller. A negro man named SIMPSON, 30; says he belongs to Mr. Villarde. A mulatto man named WILLIAM or CALEB; says he belongs to Mr. Kelvit. A griffe boy named JOHN, 18; says he belongs to Mr. Crane. A negro woman named LUCINDA, 22; says she belongs to Mr. Thompson. A bright mulatto boy named BEN, 18; says he belongs to Mr. Ransdale. A negro man named HENRY, 22; says he belongs to N. O. Draining Co. H. S. HARPER, Capt. of the Watch.

30 Nov 1839. $10 Reward. Ran away the 10th ultimo a negro girl named ANN, sometimes calls herself MARIA, about 5' 2", scars on her breast and back of the neck, caused from being cupped. N. C. LANE.

5 Dec 1839. $100 Reward. Ran away 3 weeks since a likely negro named NELSON. He is rather darker than a griffe, about 24, 5' 9", well made. As he has been on steamboats in the West and the South, he may wish to hire himself as a steward. J. A. STUART.

13 Dec 1839. $100 Reward. Ran away from the subscriber's pine wood residence, Parish of Rapides, his slave JACK. He is about 35, 5' 3". He is a Virginia negro, not very black, and is very intelligent. The above reward will be paid for his delivery to me in Alexandria, La. H. M. HYAMS.

14 Dec 1839. Ran away the 9th inst. my boy ADAM, 19 years old, 5' 5", rather slim, a dark mulatto. Any person returning said boy to me at the Planter's Hotel, New Orleans, will receive a liberal reward. S. M. LOCKHART.

14 Dec 1839. $100 Reward. Will be paid to whoever will lodge in jail the following slaves belonging to the New Orleans and Nashville Railroad company--ELLICK, black, about 28, 5' 10". RIPLEY, about 25, griffe, 5' 6". JAMES H. CALDWELL, President.

15 Dec 1839. $10 Reward. Will be given for the slave LEWIS. I gave him a pass Wednesday to see his wife who resides in the city. He is a black, about 35, 5' 6", a large scar on the side of his face and neck, and one of his hands has the appearance of having been burnt off. JOHN SMITH Jr, Master, Steamboat Norfolk.

19 Dec 1839. $100 reward will be given for delivery of the yellow boy LEVI, about 22, 5" 10", and was at the last account on board a steamboat in Red River or St. Louis trade.

26 Dec 1839. Were brought to the 2d Municipality police prison the following slaves: A negro man named JOHN DAVIS, about 33; says he belongs to Jacob Barker. A negro woman named LOUISA, about 25; says she belongs to Mr. Esinar. A negro man named APOLLO, about 20; says he belongs to Michelle Perch. A negro man named FRANK, about 20, says he belongs to Mr. Baty. A negro gril named LOUISA, about 18; says she belongs to Mr. Cantrelle. H. S. HARPER, Capt. of the Watch.

28 Dec 1839. Were brought to the 2d Municipality police prison the following slaves: a negro boy named ZEPHIR, about 12; says he belongs to Mr. Lavaselle. A mulatto man named NELSON, about 26; says he belongs to Mr. Bouligny. A negro man named WILLIAM, about 28; says he belongs to Mr. Roblain. A bright mulatto man named JOE, about 21; says he belongs to Mr. Briskey. A negro woman named BETSEY, about 30; says she belongs to Mr. Pittpain. H. S. HARPER, Capt. of the Watch.

2 Jan 1840. $50 Reward. Ran away last May a negro man named HARRY, about 23, 5' 7", dark copper color. He was formerly coachman for J. B. Digges.

15 Jan 1840. $15 Reward. Absented himself since Christmas night the mulatto boy DAVID, 34, about 5' 5", speaks English only. D. FEHRMAN.

17 Jan 1840. Were brought to the 2d Municipality police prison the following slaves: NAT, about 24, a negro, says he belongs to Mr. Lapisse. JIM, a negro, 43, says he belongs to Mr. Lafore. JACOB, a negro, 35, says he belongs to Mr. Racoste. ANDREW, a mulatto, 45, says he belongs to Pierre Dubuise. CHARLES, a mulatto, 11 or 12, says he belongs to Mr. Perks. SALLY, a negro, about 40, says she belongs to Mr.

Julien. HENRY, a griffe, about 38 or 40; says he belongs to a Mr. Smith. H. S. HARPER, Capt. of the Watch.

28 Jan 1840. $10 Reward. Ran away the 22d the griffe woman REBECCA, about 20, 5' 2", slender, 2 marks on her left cheek like deep scratches. GEORGE CARRICO.

1 Feb 1840. Were brought to the 2d Municipality police prison the following slaves: JIM, a negro, 27, says he belongs to Mr. Walsh. AMELIA, a negress, about 27, says she belongs to Mr. Roland. H. S. HARPER, Capt of the Watch.

4 Feb 1840. $50 Reward. Ran away on Dec. 12, a negro named PRINCE HARRIS, about 23, 5' 6", jet black, has a scar over his right eye. He is from Savannah, Ga., and is a ship's carpenter by trade. Has been but 3 months in this city.

21 Feb 1840. Were brought to the 2d Municipality police prison the following slaves: GEORGE, a negro, about 13, says he belongs to Mr. Nichols. JOE, a negro, 35, says he belongs to Capt. Glover. H. S. HARPER, Capt. of the Watch.

21 Feb 1840. $10 Reward. Ran away on the 3d instant, the negress LOUISA, about 35, of middle size, has a scar under her right ear. She sold dry goods in the 2d Municipality.

22 Feb 1840. Were brought to the 2d Municipality police prison the following slaves: JOHN, a negro, 25; says he belongs to Mr. Robelle. VICTOIRE, a negro, 50; says he belongs to Mr. Eusine. HENRY, a mulatto, 24; says he belongs to Mr. Humphreys. LOUISA, a negress, 13 or 14; says she belongs to Francis Leon. AUGUSTUS, a negro, 11 or 12; says he belongs to Mr. Lacoste. ELIZA, a mulatto, about 16; says she belongs to Mr. Brackenridge. ELIZABETH, a

woman, about 30; says she belongs to Mr. Edy. H. S. HARPER, Capt. of the Watch.

23 Feb 1840. Ran away from the undersigned on the 20th, a mulatto boy named ALFRED or ARCHEY, 19, 5' 6", dark, bushy hair, can read a little. M. H. DEVEREAUX.

27 Feb 1840. Were brought to the 2d Municipality police prison the following slaves: A negro woman named ROSE, about 25; says she belongs to Mr. Terbonne. ROBERT, a negro, 24; says he belongs to Mr. James. NATHAN, a negro, about 13; says he belongs to Mr. Butler. SARAH, a negress, 21; says she belongs to Capt. Osbury. H. S. HARPER, Capt. of the Watch.

4 Mar 1840. Were brought to the 2d Municipality police prison the following slaves: KITTY, a griffe woman, 43; says she belongs to Mr. Bryan. JOHN, about 23, a mulatto; says he belongs to Mr. Norfly. ANDERSON, a negro, 22; says he belongs to Mr. Harman. JAMES, a negro boy, 12; says he belongs to Mr. Rountree. A negro boy, SAM, about 12 or 13; says he belongs to Mr. Hite. H. S. HARPER, Capt. of the Watch.

4 Mar 1840. Information Wanted. By the undersigned of MADISON MEDLEY, a black man, about 23 who came to New Orleans some 4 years ago from Augusta, Bracken Co., Ky. When last heard from he was in the chain gang as a runaway slave. I now have his free papers and will give $100 for the desired information. LARKIN M. ANDERSON.

13 Mar 1840. $25 Reward. Ran away on the 8th instant a black griffe colored boy named SCOT, 28 or 30, 5' 8", speaks only English. He is a pretty good barber and worked as a

dining room servant at the City Hotel when he left. D. H. BLEASOE.

14 Mar 1840. $20 Reward. For apprehension of DAVID, a slender black, about 18, 5' 10", large hands and feet. Has a lump about the size of a bean on his left jaw below the ear. R. P. BOWIE.

18 Mar 1840. $50 Reward. Ran away the 11th inst. the negro man BOOKER, about 28, 6' tall, dark black complexion. He was a fireman on the steamer Washington and sometimes on the Mariner. His mother lives in the lower part of the city; she is a free woman. GEORGE P. SHALL.

18 Mar 1840. $20 Reward. Ran away the 14th, the negro boy SAM, aged 18, very black, bow-legged, a scar on his forehead. Was brought to this city in December by John Hall, from Vicksburg, sold to Benjamin Kendig, from whom I became the purchaser. M. T. VOORHEES.

18 Mar 1840. $25 Reward. Dr. Dalton will give above reward for delivery of his negro boy ALLEN, a black, about 14, well made and smart.

18 Mar 1840. $10 Reward. Absconded on the 3d instant, the negress DIANA, about 30, speaks French and English, slim made and good looking.

20 Mar 1840. $50 Reward. Was stolen from Col. Charles Morgan's plantation, Point Coupee, the 11th instant, by a man on a flatboat, a negro girl named MARY, about 20, rather small, bad teeth. She formerly belonged to H. C. Myers. H. N. MORISON.

22 Mar 1840. $50 Reward. Absented herself yesterday, a bright mulatto woman named ELIZA, with rather straight reddish hair, aged from 22 to 25, large in the family way. She was purchased from Mr. Nelson of Tennessee about 6 months ago. JAMES CORLIS.

31 Mar 1840. $25 Reward. Ran away from me at New Orleans, on the 3rd of March, a mulatto girl named NANCY, about 5' 2", aged 18. SARAH THOMPSON.

2 Apr 1840. $20 Reward will be paid for delivery of the mulatto boy JACOB, who absented himself on the 21st ultimo. He is about 5' 7", about 21 years old, very intelligent. P. SUMMERS.

3 Apr 1840. $10 Reward. Ran away the griffe colored boy named JARRETT, formerly belonging to Austin Woolfort of this city. He has a scar on his right cheek, is about 15 years old. P. COLLAGIANI.

5 Apr 1840. Were brought to the 2d Municipality police prison 2 slaves: PETER, about 11, a negro; says he belongs to Mr. Martee. SALLY, a negress, about 26; says she belongs to Mr. Kerr. H. S. HARPER, Capt of the Watch.

8 Apr 1840. $15 reward will be paid for apprehension of the negro woman MARIA, about 35, about 5' 2", has a scar on one of her cheeks, broad face with full set of teeth. She is a washerwoman. She is from Tennessee and has been 1 year in this city. JOHN H. VINER.

9 Apr 1840. $20 reward for the negro EDMUND, ran away from the plantation of M. & A. Reine in St. John the Baptist parish on the 26th ultimo. Edmund is 32, about 5' 5", is an

American negro, and speaks French and English. J. T. LATAPIE.

11 Apr 1840. $20 Reward will be given for apprehension of TOM, a slave boy about 5' 5", 16 or 17, very dark complexion, thin face, long arms and legs. He is a cook and is acquainted in Mobile. He may represent himself as a sailor, having once been to sea. N. H. HATCH.

16 Apr 1840. A liberal reward will be paid to whoever will lodge in any jail the griffe woman, REBECCA, about 21, 5' 2", rather slender, who absconded on the 1st inst.

16 Apr 1840. $20 Reward. To whoever will take up and secure my negro slave by name of JAGO or JAKE, who left Wednesday. He is about 6' high, speaks French and English. He formerly belonged to A. E. Charbonnet, of this city. LEON JENKINS.

18 Apr 1840. $25 Reward. Ran away the 1st inst. a negro man named ISAAC, 22, 5' 7", broad face, high forehead. JAMES R. CONWAY, St. James Parish.

19 Apr 1840. Were brought to the 2d Municipality police prison 2 slaves: a negro woman named PRICILLA, about 45 or 50; says she belongs to Mr. Conner; and a negro man named PETER, about 24; says he belongs to Mr. Lefevre. H. S. HARPER, Capt. of the Watch.

24 Apr 1840. $20 Reward. Ran away, a slave named ANDREW, 20, 5' 4", lame in one leg. He is in the habit of absenting himself. Apply to Mr. Garrison.

24 Apr 1840. Were brought to the 2d Municipality police prison the following slaves: A negro man named JIM, 22; says

he belongs to Higgins and McCluster of Mobile. A negro man named JOE, 22; says he belongs to Messrs. Lambert & Thompson. A negro man named RANDOLPH, about 32; says he belongs to John Payne of Bayou Sara. A negro boy named SAINTVILLE, 8 years old; says he belongs to Mr. Grosjean. H. S. HARPER, Capt. of the Watch.

25 Apr 1840. $10 Reward. Ran away from the subscriber the 22 inst. the mulatto boy AARON, about 15, likely, straight hair and looks like an Indian. J. LEVY.

26 Apr 1840. $50 Reward. Absconded the 25th inst. the black slave AGA, about 32, of low stature, thick lips and bad teeth. It is supposed she will attempt to get on some steamship bound for upper country, as her husband absconded about 10 months ago and is in Toronto. U. C. E. HAYES.

1 May 1840. Were brought to the 2d Municipality police prison the following slaves: A negro man named GUSTAVE, about 40; says he belongs to Mr. Delerie. A negro man named FRANCIS, about 40; says he belongs to Mr. Saule. H. S. HARPER, Capt. of the Watch.

3 May 1840. $5 Reward. Will be paid for apprehension of the negress MILLIE, about 50, a cook, washer and ironer. Has been in the habit of working about the city. Has a scar on her left leg and one under her left eye. Formerly owned by James Brown, and now the property of Ann Mutter.

3 May 1840. $10 Reward. Ran away from the subscriber the 26th ult. the slave LOUICENE or LOUISIANNE, about 20, a griffe, about 5', heavy eyebrows, front teeth all decayed. She speaks English only. F. A. LEMOYNE.

7 May 1840. $10 Reward. Ran away Sunday last, a negro woman (griffe) named SIDNEY, 28, and quite stout. Her front teeth are somewhat decayed. She speaks low and modest. J. A. STUART.

10 May 1840. Were brought to the 2d Municipality police prison the following slaves: A negro woman named REBECCA, about 60; says she belongs to Mr. Beard. A negro boy named PETER, about 10; says he belongs to Mr. Marty. A griff man named HENRY, about 25; says he belongs to C. Chiappel. H. S. HARPER, Capt. of the Watch.

16 May 1840. The negro man ROBERT has been missing since Friday last. He is lame, having one leg amputated above the knee, and uses a crutch. J. S. TURNELL.

22 May 1840. Ran away from the 1st Municipality vegetable market on the 19th inst. the American negro GEORGE, aged 30, 5' 9", speaks French and English, dark complexion. F. E. FAZENDE.

27 May 1840. $25 Reward. Ran away the 23 inst. a dark freckled mulatto named THOMAS TAYLOR; has been badly ruptured and may have on Warner's Patent Truss. He is about 26, 5' 10" tall. He was purchased in April of Mr. Hickey, of Natchez, Miss., and has a wife living here. He ran away in May, 1839, and was found in jail in Natchez, also last October, and was taken up in Baton Rouge. There he stated he belonged to Thomas Mills of New Orleans. THOMAS B. WINSTON.

27 May 1840. Were brought to the 2d Municipality police prison the following slaves: A negro girl named MARGARET, about 12 or 13; says she belongs to Antoine Valette. A boy named SAM, 14; says he belongs to Mr.

Nicaud. A mulatto man named LEWIS, about 30; says he belongs to Mr. Christian. A negro man named LOUIS, about 22; says he belongs to Mr. Fortier. A negro woman named ELIZABETH, about 25; says she belongs to Mr. Fourchi. A negro man named DANIEL, about 28; says he belongs to Mr. Blanchard. H. S. HARPER, Capt. of the Watch.

29 May 1840. $15 Reward. Left the house of the subscriber, the 25th inst. the negress POLLY or PAULINE; she is about 35, slight made, 5' 3", and speaks French and English. She was formerly owned by Doctor Luzenberg.

29 May 1840. $15 Reward. Ran away on the 18th the negro boy HILAYE, 5' 3", stout built, a mark from a burn on his breast. Known in the city as a cart driver. JOHN CREON.

31 May 1840. $100 Reward. For arrest of the slave FREDERICK, a griffe, aged 30, 5' 11", a dray driver in the city for the last 2 years. He ran away the 28th, and is believed to have taken with him his wife, a black woman belonging to Mr. C. Genoir, and likewise their daughter, 6 or 7, very smart for her age and cuppled. FRERET BROTHERS.

31 May 1840. $25 Reward for delivery of a Creole negress, CHARLOTTE, about 34, absent more than 2 months. She is black, speaks French and some English. She has a free colored man as her husband. N. N. WILKINSON.

31 May 1840. $100 Reward for securing in jail a slave named TOM, about 18, 5' 6", dark complexion; says he is a free man and calls himself Thomas Philips. I have another boy named BILL, a runaway, 18, 5' 5", very dark--he ran away from Vicksburg 2 weeks ago on board a steamboat. The boys were purchased by me in Mobile 2 months ago. N. W. HATCH.

12 Jun 1840. Were brought to the 2d Municipality police prison: A negro man named WILLIAM, about 26; says he belongs to Mr. Valmaur. A negro man named WESTLEY, about 32; says he belongs to Mr. Norton. A negro man named CHARLES, about 28; says he belongs to Mr. Norman. H. S. HARPER, Capt. of the Watch.

14 Jun 1840. $25 Reward. Ran away on the 8th of Nov. last the griffe slave MARY ANNE, 45, 5' 6"; was formerly owned by Nicholas Murray. R. W. ELLIOTT.

24 Jun 1840. $50 Reward. Ran away 4 months ago a griffe girl, about 5' high, aged 15, named CAROLINE. Her mother lives at Huntsville. BRIDGET HENETTY.

24 Jun 1840. Ran away about the 24th of September, 1839, two negroes--BOB and VINA, his wife. He is of dark complexion, 30, about 6' high; calls himself ROBERT GILLMORE. VINA is of ordinary stature, dark complexion, about 27 or 28. Bob was raised by George Wells, late of Hinds Co., Miss., and Vina in St. Louis, Mo. I will pay $100 for each of them. MORDECAI BALDWIN, Baldwin's Ferry, Hinds Co., Miss.

30 Jun 1840. $50 Reward. Ran away June 1, a likely negro man named JEFFERSON, a first rate blacksmith, about 170 lbs. He obtained free papers, one in French, one in English, the latter representing him by the name of Jo Wilson, signed by --- --- Butler, stating he purchased himself for the sum of $1,500. IRVIN QUIN, Holmesville, Pike Co., Miss.

4 Jul 1840. $10 Reward. Will be paid for apprehension of a griffe or light colored man named JOB, middle size, about 30; has run as a steward or cook on some of the upriver boats last season. Has probably been enticed away by his wife, a free

quadroon, who lately lived in Vicksburg. DAVID JOHN ROGERS.

7 Jul 1840. $200 Reward. Ran away at Canton, Madison Co., Miss., on 20 June, the mulatto boy PAYTON, 16, 5' 5", very likely. He was last seen at Vicksburg. W. A. FORT, Canton, Miss.

7 Jul 1840. $10 Reward for apprehension of the negro girl MARY, about 35, dark griffe, and her 2 children, AMELIA, about 6, dark griffe, the other about 2, a mulatto. T. WILLIAMS.

9 Jul 1840. Were brought to the 2d Municipality police prison the following slaves: A negro boy named HENRY, about 19; says he belongs to Mr. Storus. A negro woman, LUCY, about 36; says she belongs to Mr. Carter of Baton Rouge. A negro man named BOB, about 24; says he belongs to Judge Butler. A negro man named PETER, about 35; says he belongs to Mr. Dale. A negro man named WILLIAM, about 45; says he belongs to Mr. Laran. A negro woman named SARAH, 18; says she belongs to Miss. Porter. H. S. HARPER, Capt. of the Watch.

21 Jul 1840. $10 Reward. Ran away the 17th inst. a negro girl, HANNAH, about 14, low stature, two fronth teeth out. PETER GERNON.

21 Jul 1840. $20 Reward. for 2 negroes who ran away the 19th, formerly belonging to John Bertrand, of this city. SAM is about 24, a mulatto. He is about 6 feet high. EDWARD, about 28 is black, about 5' 6". DAVID BARBOUR.

28 JUL 1840. $10 Reward. Absented himself on the 26th, the black boy MACE or MASON, about 6' 8", a small scar on the bridge of his nose. CHARLES DIAMOND.

8 Aug 1840. $20 Reward. Will be given for the slave HARRY, formerly owned by Mr. H. P. Peck of Catahoula; about 24, 5' 7", heavy built, slow gait, scars across his nose, lip and left eye. SIDDLE & STEWART.

6 Aug 1840. $10 Reward. Absconded from the subscriber on 29th of July, the black boy GEORGE, about 5' 9", rather slim built. He was formerly owned by Mr. Morton. J. A. BAILEY.

6 Aug 1840. $25 Reward for delivery of the slave CLAIBORNE, a dark mulatto, aged 25, who absconded 29th July. Claiborne is stout, muscular, about 5' 8", with a sullen look. He has been on board the steamboat Claiborne and others for some time. J. A. BEARD.

6 Aug 1840. Were brought to the 2d Municipality police prison the following slaves: A negro man named ELLICK, about 25; says he belongs to Mr. Meads. A light mulatto woman named SARAH, about 19; says she belongs to Mr. Hughes. H. S. HARPER, Capt. of the Watch.

8 Aug 1840. $100 Reward. Stolen or ran off from my Astorniah plantation on the Mississippi River about 10 miles above Fort Adams, my negro boy GREEN, about 19, very dark complexion, remarkably white teeth, bushy head of hair, generally parted. He is about 5' 7" high. WILLIAM STAMP, Woodville, Miss.

12 Aug 1840. Were brought to the 2d Municipality police prison the following slaves. A negro man named WILLIAM, about 35; says he belongs to Mr. Whiting. A negro woman

named MARY about 35; says she belongs to Mr. Hopkins. A negro boy named HECTOR, about 18 or 20; says he belongs to Mr. Delerie. H. S. HARPER, Capt. of the Watch.

13 Aug 1840. $10 Reward. Will be paid for the griffe boy named WILLIAM, 18, about 5' 9", who absconded the 10th inst. He was previously owned in Port Gibson, Miss., where he has said he has a wife.

13 Aug 1840. $20 Reward for a dark mulatto boy named BOB, about 5' 7 or 8", who ran away on the 10th. EDWARD SMITH.

20 Aug 1840. Were brought to the 2d Municipality police prison the following slaves: A negro boy named PRIMUS, about 35; says he belongs to Mr. Sterling. A negro boy named LEONARD, about 13; says he belongs to Mr. Davis. A negro woman named BETSY, about 25; says she belongs to Mr. Smith. A negro woman named SARAH; says she belongs to Mr. Perro. A griffe woman named SALLY; says she belongs to Mr. Avard. H. S. HARPER, Capt. of the Watch.

22 Aug 1840. $10 Reward. Ran away from me the boy RUBEN, about 5' 6", copper colored, is ruptured and wears a truss. Had on when he left, a check shirt, duck trousers, and an iron collar. WILLIAM SITICOTON.

23 Aug 1840. $15 Reward. Will be paid for delivery of the slave KESIAH, about 23, who absconded from my house on the 19th of August. She is stout and muscular, is about 5' 10". She was originally from Mississippi and has been in the city only 10 days. JOHN JAY KELLOGG.

29 Aug 1840. $10 Reward. Ran away on the 25th inst. a negro man named CHARLES, a Guinea negro about 40. Has straight

mark on his cheek and several on his breast, some front teeth missing. Speaks broken English. C. H. KENNEDY.

3 Sep 1840. Were brought to the 2d Municipality police prison the following slaves: A negro man named ADAM, about 45; says he belongs to Mr. Greene. A negro boy named ASINER, about 19; says he belongs to Mr. Jaulle. A negro woman named ELIZABETH, about 35; says she belongs to Mr. Lepper. A negro man named JOHN, about 25; says he belongs to Mr. Stone, of Mississippi. A negro man named DAVID, about 30; says he belongs to Mr. Richards; he is marked with smallpox.

8 Sep 1840. NOTICE. John Keller secreted or harbored with some friends of his, 2 young negroes belonging to the succession of Sarah Baum, deceased--BILL, a negro boy about 9, and a girl about 7 named PRISSA. It is notorious and a matter of record that said Keller once before secreted a negro belonging to the same succession. I will pay $15 to any person who will deliver to me the 2 said negroes. THOMAS POWELL, Dative Testamentary, Exr of Sarah Baum, Dec'd.

8 Sep 1840. $10 Reward will be paid for arrest of my negress MARY, who absconded on the 5th inst. She is about 5' tall, aged about 33 years, griffe colored, and has the name of H. RINNE marked on her right arm. D. S. GREGORY.

9 Sep 1840. $5 Reward for the negress NANCY, about 30, about 6' high of a slender stature. Said slave ran away on the 2d inst. C. F. THONKE.

13 Sep 1840. $20 Reward. Ran away on the 7th inst. a black boy named CASIMER, slim made, about 5' 5", 22 years old, calls himself free. He is a Creole of Louisiana, is a bootblack, and has a cut on his left ear. P. HOWARD.

17 Sep 1840. Was brought to the 2d Municipality police prison a negro slave named GRANVILLE, about 35; says he belongs to Mr. Bird; has a defect in one eye. H. S. HARPER, Capt. of the Watch.

19 Sep 1840. $10 Reward. Ran away the 11th, the boy SOLOMON, about 5' 11", 19, a large scar on his breast from a burn. Has a round bald spot on the top of his head from carrying mortar buckets. A. G. WILSON.

23 Sep 1840. $10 Reward. Will be paid for delivery to me of the girl LUCY who ran off on the 17th inst. She is a griffe, 17, 5' 3", speaks English and a little French. J. B. P. MAXENT.

29 Sep 1840. Were brought to the 2d Municipality police prison the following slaves: A negro boy named FRANCIS, 10; says he belongs to Theofile Cavalier. A negro man named MOSES, about 30; says he belongs to Mr. Drausia Labranche. H. S. HARPER, Capt. of the Watch.

1 Oct 1840. $10 Reward. Ran away the 28th inst. the black boy JOHN LEWIS, about 4' 6", thick set, no front teeth, 19 years old. Speaks French and English.

1 Oct 1840. $10 Reward. Ran away about the 23d ultimo my negro boy ELLIS, very black, about 40, nearly 6 feet high. Speaks English only. P. SHEILS.

2 Oct 1840. $20 Reward. Ran away the 3d ultimo, the negress MARIA, about 5' 9", aged 35, speaks only English. Also absconded the negro HUBBARD, Maria's husband, about 30, 5' 8". J. W. COLLINS

2 Oct 1840. $10 Reward. Ran away the 23d ultimo, a negro boy ELLIS, very black, about 40, speaks English only. P. SHEILS.

2 Oct 1840. $20 Reward. For a yellow wench who left the premises at No. 150 Camp st. on Saturday with the view of getting her clothes, CAROLINE JORDAIN, 27 years old, often passes as free.

2 Oct 1840. $20 Reward. Will be paid to any person who will lodge in any city jail the negro man named JOHN, who ran away about 5 weeks ago. He is short, has thin shoulders, and fine hair which he takes pride in dressing, being a barber. He formerly belonged to Amos Webb in Attakapas, and a Thomas B. Lee of this city. He was employed last year at a barber shop opposite the St. Charles Hotel. MRS. E. LEVFEBRE.

7 Oct 1840. Were brought to the 2d Municipality police prison the following slaves: A mulatto man named WILL, about 35 or 40; says he belongs to Mr. Johnson. A negro boy named WILLIAM, 10 or 12 years old; says he belongs to Mr. Martin White. H. S. HARPER, Capt. of the Watch.

9 Oct 1840. $10 Reward. Ran away from me on the 7th inst. the negro girl SARAH ANN, about 18, stout built, rather pleasant countenance. W. E. TURNER.

15 Oct 1840. $10 Reward. Ran away on the 11th inst. a negro slave named LOUIS, formerly belonging to Planters Hotel in Canal St. He is about 5' 5", a little marked with the smallpox, not very dark color. MIGUEL MARTE.

17 Oct 1840. Was committed to jail in Chicot Co., Arkansas, the 3d of June last a runaway slave who says his name is JOHN, and that he belongs to John Battiste, a butcher in New

Orleans, who purchased him from Mr. Churchill of Louisville, Ky. He is black, about 20, 5' 6". WILFORD GARNER, Sheriff.

22 Oct 1840. Were brought to the 2d Municipality police prison the following slaves. A small griffe named HARRIS, about 12; says he belongs to Mr. Egan. A negro boy named HARRISON, about 10; says he belongs to Mr. Egan. A negro man named JERRY, 25; says he belongs to Mr. Dubuque. H. S. HARPER, Capt. of the Watch.

27 Oct 1840. $15 Reward. Will be given to whoever will lodge in jail the mulatto man WILLIAM, who ran off yesterday. He is yellow, round face, middle stature. W. W. WILKINSON.

2 Nov 1840. $20 Reward. RUNAWAY--my boy AARON has been gone some weeks; he is 27, 5' 7", a painter by trade. B. BAGGETT.

2 Nov 1840. $100 Reward. Ran away from me a slave named DELIA, about 26, 5' 5". H. F. WADE.

4 Nov 1840. Were brought to the 2d Municipality police prison the following slaves: A griffe boy named EPHRAIM, about 25; says he belongs to Mr. Reason Bowie; is about 5' 11" high; says he ran away about 6 months ago. A black boy named PETERSON, about 40; says he belongs to William Issacs of the Island of Tautola; about 5' 10" and marked with the smallpox. H. S. HARPER, Capt. of the Watch.

15 Nov 1840. Were brought to the 2d Municipality police prison the following slaves: A mulatto boy named DICK, about 20; says he belongs to Mr. Dowdy of Tennessee. A negro boy about 19, 5' 7" tall, calls himself JIM; says he

belongs to Mr. Otwig. A negro boy 10 years old who calls himself CHARLES; says he belongs to Mr. Aicard. A negro boy about 11 calling himself HENRY; says he belongs to Mr. Gustaffe. H. S. HARPER, Capt. of the Watch.

19 Nov 1840. $20 Reward. Will be paid for apprehension of the boy JOHN, who ran away the 18th ult. He was bought from Daniel McCann, of Missouri, a short time since; he is of small size, black complexion, smooth skin, 2 front teeth out. Pretends to be a cook. Was for some time in Dr. Stone's hospital. Speaks English only. CHARLES A. JACOBS.

20 Nov 1840. $10 Reward. Will be paid to any person who will bring to 27 Tchoupitoulas St. a negro girl about 13 years old, very black, rough skin, quite sprightly, of short stature, named MARTHA.

25 Nov 1840. Were brought to the 2d Municipality police prison the following slaves: A negro boy named ABRAHAM, about 10; says he belongs to Mr. Wilkins. A negro boy about 11, named FRANCIS; says he belongs to Mr. Cuviller. A griffe girl about 15, named MARY; says she belongs to Mr. Batiste Delony. A mulatto man named ANDERSON, 20; says he belongs to Mr. Pierre Dubois. A negro girl named FANNY, about 20; says she belongs to Mr. Soby. H. S. HARPER, Capt. of the Watch.

1 Dec 1840. $20 Reward for delivery of my negro woman, MARIA, ran away yesterday. She is of dark complexion, middle size, is about 34. SAMUEL BELL.

3 December 1840. $25 Reward. Ran away, the boy GRIFFIN or GARRISON; he formerly belonged to Richard Murphy of this city. He is about 5' 8 or 9", 27, a very light mulatto (in fact, some persons would mistake him for a white man);

straight hair, slight scar on his chin; has lost a tooth. He has some knowledge of the carpenter's trade, painter's trade, and whitewasher's trade. A. E. FORBUSH.

4 December 1840. $20 Reward for the apprehension and delivery to me of a bright mulatto boy named JOHN, about 27, 5' 8 or 10", full face and smooth skin, rather inclined to corpulency. JOSEPH A. BEARD.

5 Dec 1840. $50 Reward. Stolen from Bay of St. Louis, Wednesday last a very light mulatto child, about 3 years old, a small mark in the corner of one eye, black hair. The above reward will be paid for the child and apprehension of the thief, or $25 for the child if delivered to Bay of St. Louis to Madame Johnson. All persons are cautioned not to buy a child of the above description.

15 Dec 1840. $10 Reward. Ran away from me on Saturday, my slave MARY ANN, about 22 years old; has a slight scar near the left eye and one on her left shoulder. She is of middle height, and speaks French and English fluently. If the above slave returns home, all will be forgiven and no punishment inflicted on her. MRS. TIMMONEY.

18 Dec 1840. $20 Reward. Ran away the 15th inst. my boy LEONARD, 22, black, speaks French and English, formerly belonged to Mrs. Tracy of this city. J. ANDREWS.

18 Dec 1840. $25 Reward. Ran away the 5th inst. a yellow boy, JOHN PERRY, 22, 5' 4", lame in his left leg. He has lived in St. Louis, Mo., but for the last 7 or 8 years he has lived in Louisiana, and lately purchased from Henry Bradley, St. Mary parish. GEORGE P. SHALL.

19 Dec 1840. $10 Reward. Ran away on Sunday a black boy named HENRY, 14. C. H. TANNY.

19 Dec 1840. $20 Reward for HAMILTON, a dark griffe negro, about 5' 10", 40 years old, well made and very straight, wants all his teeth except two in front, speaks English very imperfectly. Belongs to JOHN DUGGAN.

25 Dec 1840. Ran away on the 17th of last month a negro woman about 23, 5' 5", broad shouldered, smooth, black face, talks French and English. Formerly belonged to Mr. Wilkinson, near the Union Cotton Press. Her name is JUDY or JULIA. DANIEL PHILLIPS.

30 Dec 1840. $10 Reward. Ran away the 27th instant the slave woman VENICE, about 35, low stature, speaks French and English. JOHN HEINE.

30 Dec 1840. Commanded to my care, on 13 Dec., a negro man who says his name is JOHN and that he belongs to Mary Jane, a Creole living in New Orleans. He is copperish color, and is about 23, 5' 3". MILLER IRVIN, Sheriff, Helena, Phillips Co., Arkansas.

1 Jan 1841. $20 Reward. Ran away on 28 Dec., the mulatto woman CATHERINE, about 24, speaks French and English. H. CZARNOWSKE.

3 Jan 1841. Were brought to the 2d Municipality police prison the following slaves. A negro woman named JULIANNE, about 40; says she belongs to Mr. Lappalit. A negro man called ALEX, about 25; says he belongs to Mr. Raphale of Bayou Lafouche. A mulatto boy named TOBY, 10 or 11; says he belongs to Henry Laudun. A negro man named SANDY, 25, says he belongs to Mr. Preston. A mulatto boy named

SAM, 18; says he belongs to Mr. Milligan. H. S. HARPER, Capt. of the Watch.

12 Jan 1841. $40 Reward. Ran away from the bakery on Bourbon St. the negro man, FRANCOIS or CHAPEAU, belonging to Mr. Nicaud. He is about 24, 5'.

12 Jan 1841. $5 Reward for the negro boy PETER, who left me on the 10th instant. He is about 5', a small piece out of his left ear. K. KRITZBERGER, Lafayette, La.

16 Jan 1841. $10 Reward. Ran away the 11th, the negro boy PHILIP, about 25, 5' 7 or 8". Formerly belonged to Mr. Dobb, in Lafayette. JAMES PHILLIPS.

16 Jan 1841. $20 Reward. Will be paid for arrest of my boy DAN, a well known drayman in the city, 5' 6", slender, speaks English and French, a scar on his face. J. FOX.

16 Jan 1841. Were brought to the 2d Municipality police prison the following slaves: A negro woman named AMELIA, about 24; says she belongs to Mr. Coste. A negro man named JACK, about 26; says he belongs to Mr. Duvall. A negro boy named WILLIAM, about 18 or 20; says he belongs to Mr. Forreste. A negro woman named MARGUERITE, about 35; says she belongs to Mr. Fonteroy. H. S. HARPER, Capt. of the Watch.

20 Jan 1841. $10 Reward. Ran away, the boy HENRY, a griffe, aged 38, stout built, about 5' 9" tall, has a scar on his right cheek. JOSEPH B. CARSON.

24 Jan 1841. $10 Reward. Ran away on the 21st, the black boy NED, about 35 or 50, 5' 6", a scar near one eye. Whoever

returns above slave to me shall receive the above reward. OWEN D. EGAN.

28 Jan 1841. Were brought to the 2d Municipality police prison the following slaves: A negro man named FIELD, about 22; says he belongs to Mr. Woodville. A griff man named HENRY, about 35; says he belongs to Mr. Croisi. A negro man named JOHN RICH, about 5' 6" tall; says he belongs to Mr. Williams. H. S. HARPER, Capt. of the Watch.

29 Jan 1841. $10 Reward. Ran away from the subscriber in Mobile on the 18th inst. FERDINAND SMITH, a bright mulatto boy, about 20, 5' 6 or 7" high; is a tailor by trade. Has a scar on his right cheek. He is very intelligent and can read and write. C. W. CHURCHILL.

3 Feb 1841. $25 Reward. Ran away a week since, 2 slaves--a mulatto man about 6', 40 years old, named PHILIP, and EPHRAIM, about 10. They were attached to the suit of J. F. Mosby vs. John G. Chalmers. J. F. MOSBY.

10 Feb 1841. I have in my possession a negro man named EPHRAM, who says he was sold by me in 1837 to William Johnson, of Natchez, Miss., and that said Johnson was killed in a late storm there. He is about 22, 5' 6". B. C. EATON.

10 Feb 1841. $25 Reward. Will be paid for recovery of a yellow boy, DICK. DANIEL GREEN, Grand Gulf, Miss.

20 Feb 1841. $10 Reward. Ran away a few days ago the griffe boy HENRY, 5' 8", a scar on his right cheek. JOSEPH B. CARSON.

20 Feb 1841. $10 Reward. Ran away on Friday last, the black boy RANDLE, about 22, about 5' 10", has lost one of his front

teeth. He limps a little. He formerly belonged to George A. Botts. JAMES WRIGHT.

26 Feb 1841. $15 Reward will be paid for apprehension of the negro man called JOHN CUNNINGHAM, who ran away last week. He is below middle size, of smooth black skin, speaks English and French, and pretends to be a good cook and is thought to have lost one of his fingers.

5 Mar 1841. $20 Reward. Ran away from their mistress, Madame Marguéretta Jardell, the negress PELAGIE and the mulatto PIERRE, her son. O. B. HILL.

5 Mar 1841. $25 Reward. Will be given for the mulatto boy LEWIS, about 25, 5' 6", speaks English only. He has been a dray cart driver here for some time. JULES A. BLANC.

5 Mar 1841. $5 Reward. Ran away on the 1st inst. a mulatto woman named CRESY, about 5', 28 years old. CHARLES KERNER.

5 Mar 1841. $10 Reward for the black boy MASON, 25, who ran away last month. CHARLES DIAMOND.

11 Mar 1841. $50 Reward. Ran away yesterday a good looking, stout negro named WILLIAM GREEN, 29, bought from Capt. George Taylor.

11 Mar 1841. $50 reward will be paid for delivery to me in Salem, Ky., of the negro boy EDMUND, property of Jesse Padon, deceased, who ran away from custody of Dr. D. B. Sanders of Smithland, Ky., Jan. 15, last. He is about 5' 6", about 25, yellowish complexion. JAMES L. ALCORN, Exo. of Jesse Padon.

11 Mar 1841. Ran away from me in Donaldsonville, La., Feb. 26, a mulatto creole boy, WILLIAM. He speaks French and English, is about 20, 5' 7". He was purchased some months since of Mr. Nadaud of New Orleans. HENRY W. MILLER.

14 Mar 1841. $5 Reward. Ran away my boy PETER, about 17, with an iron collar around his neck. A piece of his left ear is off. CASPAR KRISBEGER.

24 Mar 1841. For the arrest and confinement in jail of the boy EDWARD COOK, I will pay $20 reward. He is a likely mulatto about 19 years old. He ran away on the 22d inst. S. F. STATLER.

26 Mar 1841. $20 Reward will be paid for apprehension of the boy SOLOMON who absconded on the 20th inst. He is about 5' 5" tall. PARK & RYAN.

26 Mar 1841. $5 Reward. For the negro boy GEORGE, who ran away on the 22d inst. He is about 20 and of dark complexion. WILLIAM WATSON.

4 Apr 1841. $10 Reward. Ran away the 13th ult. a black woman named MARTHA, of low stature, about 38, and quite lame. Is supposed to be harbored by some of the washerwomen of the city, as she is superior washer. GEORGE FLAGG.

7 Apr 1841. $50 reward will be paid to any person who will secure in prison in New Orleans or Lafayette the yellow woman called LETTITIA, commonly called Let, about 23, large, tall and well looking. JESSE HARRISON.

18 Apr 1841. $10 Reward. For delivery of the mulatto boy JACK, about 13, straight black hair and round features (might be mistaken for a white boy). J. S. CROCKETT.

21 Apr 1841. Inveigled away from me the negro man WESTLEY, 22, light complexion, about 175 lbs. He was carried off by one Mary Roberts, of ill fame, to appropriate him for her use as a servant and as her husband. She has changed her name to Robertson. She was pursued to Mobile, Ala., and left Harris Co., Ga., on the steamboat P. Miller, bound for Arkansas. BENJAMIN HENRY, Harris Co., Ga.

23 Apr 1841. $10 Reward. For my negro girl HARRIETT, who ran away the 15th inst. She is 5' 5" high, 19 years old, and has a scar on her right cheek and a mole on the left side of her chin. The above reward will be paid on her delivery to any jail or to Mrs. Jane Railey, Commercial Hotel.

25 Apr 1841. Lost or Stolen. Information on a negro girl named MILLY, about 19, will be thankfully received at Madame Wooster's, 126 Canal St.

27 Apr 1841. $15 Reward. Ran away 6 weeks ago from the boarding home of Mrs. Page, a griffe man named WILLIAM PRICE, about 30 or 35, about 6' high, active and well built, a good cook and gardener. R. N. OGDEN, his master.

1 May 1841. $10 Reward. Ran away on the 30th of April last, the mulatto boy NORVELL, 19, 5' 5" high, long bushy hair, sometimes parted in the middle. Whoever returns him to David Middleton at the National Hotel shall receive the above reward.

11 May 1841. $250 Reward. Ran away on the 25th ult. a negro boy named CORNELIUS, 17 years old, copper colored, with a

scar on his upper lip, smart and intelligent. He has been with race horses all his life. When he left he took with him $250 in New Orleans funds. JOHN G. PERRY.

12 May 1841. $10 Reward. Ran away yesterday a negro woman named MATILDA, aged about 30, 4' 7", small features, speaks French and English. Also, a negro boy named WILLIAM, 14, 4' 4" high, also speaks French and English. Apply this newspaper.

22 May 1841. $100 Reward. Ran away from the subscriber, near Raymond, county seat of Hinds county, Miss., on the 28th of December last, a negro boy of light complexion, spare built, about 17 years old, named ISAAC. He was owned by Mrs. Fretwell of Vicksburg, Miss. A. ERWIN.

25 May 1841. MISSING since the 10th inst. the negress AGGY, of small stature, very black, thin face, about 40. She formerly belonged to John Hoey, saddler. Whoever will return her to Mrs. E. Johnston, 123 Casscalvo St., will receive $5 Reward.

27 May 1841. $100 Reward. Ran away on the 18th inst. the mulatto slave named WILLIAM, 36, 5' 10", slender form, hair long and curly. MADAME HAWLEY, his mistress.

1 Jun 1841. $25 Reward will be paid for apprehension of my boy TOM, who absconded from 24 Royal St. last evening. Said boy is about 30, about 5' 8", and very black. F. M. FISK.

2 Jun 1841. The public are warned not to purchase or trade for the slave named HENRY. CYRUS PARKHURST.

2 Jun 1841. $100 Reward. Ran away the 10 inst. the negro man MOSES, about 28, 5' 5", light black complexion, some

front teeth out, a slit in each ear. He is intelligent and can read well. He is an old hand at running away. He was purchased last spring as a jail runaway in Perry Co., Ala.

6 Jun 1841. $50 Reward. Ran away the 4th a negro man named WALLACE, stout built, 6', nearly black, fine curly hair, about 24. I purchased him about 3 months ago from Theophile Freeman who brought him from the District of Columbia. WILLIAM H. AVERY.

9 Jun 1841. Ran away from the steamer Pekin on the 6th, the mulatto slave PATRICK, about 6'. Speaks French and English. He is a cook. GEORGE W. SQUIRES.

15 Jun 1841. $10 Reward. Ran away the 5th inst. the slave ELIZA. She is middle size, griff, with very large eyes. GREGORY BYRNE.

18 Jun 1841. $20 Reward will be paid for the apprehension of the slave MARIE or MARY, who absconded 5 months since. Marie formerly belonged to Mr. Tabony, of New Orleans, and speaks French and English. She is of common stature, about 28 years old. She is a good cook, washer and ironer. She took with her, her child, a mulatto boy about 7 months old. C. H. TANEY.

22 Jun 1841. $5 Reward. Ran away on the 14th inst. the griffe girl ELIZABETH, between 14 and 15, 4' 6 or 8", stout built. She has a scar on her cheek and has very hard hands caused by being frostbitten. Apply 15 Esplanade St.

24 Jun 1841. $20 Reward. Ran away from my plantation in the parish of Iberville, a mulatto man named RAPHAEL, a creole of this city, about 30, well made, 6 feet high. He formerly drove a cart in the city. GEORGE A. BOTTS.

29 Jun 1841. Ran away from my plantation in East Feliciana parish a negro man named MINOR, about 20, 5' 7". He was brought to New Orleans 3 years ago from Virginia. GEORGE KELLER.

29 Jun 1841. Ran away the 27th from the plantation of Auguste Reggio, Plaquemines parish, the following slaves. LUKE, 25, 5' 7", very black. ENOCH, 22, 5' 6". ABRAHAM, a griffe, 18. They were bought last month from James Holliday.

30 Jun 1841. $30 Reward. Absconded about 10 days ago, the negro boy DAN, belonging to Madam Fox, about 5' 8", 24 years old; speaks French and English. He has a scar on his left hand. He has been driving a dray for the last 2 years. E. L. TRACY.

7 Jul 1841. Ran away on the 18th, ult., the negro boy SCYE, about 20, 5' 6". It is supposed he absented himself because he does not want to be sold. MARY SPEARING.

7 Jul 1841. $50 Reward will be paid for ALFRED, a mulatto man who ran away from me last week. He is 24, about 5' 7", with a small scar above one eye. He is very stout, speaks French and English, and is remarkably intelligent. He reads and writes and is a good bricklayer. He has passed in Cincinnati as a freeman, under the assumed name of HARRISON SPEARS. J. A. BEARD.

7 Jul 1841. $25 Reward. Ran away on the 24th, ult., the girl MARY or JANE. She is of griffe color, about 19, full face and large lips, and has the mark of a whip under one eye and on the back of her neck. G. VANDRELL.

7 Jul 1841. $20 Reward. Ran away from my plantation a mulatto man named RAPHAEL, a creole, 6 feet tall. GEORGE A. BOTTS.

7 Jul 1841. $10 Reward for the slave ELIZA, middle size, griffé. GREGORY BYRNE.

10 Jul 1841. $20 Reward. Ran away from Col. Proctor's plantation, Terre aux Boef, 4 months ago, a negro man named WILLIAM BEE, 35, 5' 5".

15 Jul 1841. $10 Reward. Ran away a negro named ROBERT, about 5' 6", dark complexion. H. F. WADE.

15 Jul 1841. Ran away from the plantation of Auguste Reggio, parish of Plaquemines, on the 12th the following slaves. LUKE, 25, black, 6' 7". JACKSON, 26, 6'. They were purchased from James Holliday.

15 Jul 1841. $20 Reward. Absconded a negro man named GEORGE SYPHAX, black, 5' 8", formerly belonged to W. M. LAMBETH, afterwards to T. B. Winston.

16 Jul 1841. $10 Reward. For the arrest of an old gray-haired mulatto man, DALGER, 5' 6". He frequently passes by the name of Baptiste and is known among the negroes in the city as a physician.

16 Jul 1841. $50 Reward. Absented himself in April last the negro CHARLES, 5' 6", speaks English and French. Formerly belonged to Mr. Huey and now belongs to the succession of William Crane of Livaudias.

20 Jul 1841. $20 Reward. Ran away on the 18th inst. the negress LOUISA, about 35. Has a scar under her right eye. Is

of middle size. She is supposed to be concealed by some person in Lafayette, as she was once taken there already.

21 Jul 1841. $50 Reward. Ran away or stolen from me on the 18th of May last, a mulatto boy named CORNELIUS, about 23, 6' high, 175 lbs., stout made, one tooth out on the left side. I am inclined to believe he has been decoyed off by some abolitionist scoundrel. $25 will be paid for the boy alone, or $50 on conviction of the thief. WILLIAM C. GOODRICH.

28 Jul 1841. $50 Reward. Absconded from the residence of S. L. Levy, on 19 June, a mulatto man named JAMES. He is about 5' 8 or 9", rather round shouldered, civil and intelligent in speech. He belonged to Augustin Frederick of Augusta, Ga., and was sent to this city aboard the schooner Richard Baker for consignment to the undersigned for sale. ABERNATHY, HANNA & KIRKMAN.

28 Jul 1841. Ran away from me the 14th last, the slave MARY ANN, about 32, of a griffe color, 5' 4 or 5", slender built, hard of hearing, and is inclined to intemperance. F. SOMMERS.

11 Aug 1841. $50 reward. Absconded from the steamboat Athenian in June a yellow boy named ALFORD, 20, 6' tall. I purchased him in Missouri and sold him to Francis Pleasance of Bayou Lafourche. THOMAS HUNDLEY.

11 Aug 1841. $500 reward for the mulatto boys WILLIAM and GEORGE BRADLEY. George is about 30, hair thick. William is about 22, 5' 8", and very white. A. P. WILLIAMS, Alexandria, La.

17 Aug 1841. $20 Reward. Absconded on the 18th, the griffe boy HENRY, 28, 6 feet tall, plays the clarinet and viola tolerably, very light complexion, very gentlemanly, speaks

English and can read and write. He is a carpenter by trade, and sometimes works as a barber. THEOPHILE FREEMAN.

17 Aug 1841. $5 Reward. Ran away 3 weeks since the black girl NANCY, 30, has but few teeth. C. F. THONKE.

22 Aug 1841. $100 Reward. Ran away from me, living in Woodford County, Ky., on the 18th inst. a yellow girl named LOUISA, but commonly called Leek, about 15, handsomely formed, and very likely, with long bushy hair and medium build. It is probable she was taken away on the steamboat Col. Woods, which left New Orleans for Louisville on the 28th of July. WILLIAM WOODS.

27 Aug 1841. $20 Reward. Will be paid for apprehension of the slave PRIMUS, who ran away from the steamer Persian on the 18th inst. He was a fireman on board. He is black and about 5' 8". The large toe on his left foot has been cut off. JESSE HART.

11 Sep 1841. Committed to jail in Carroll parish a negro boy named JIM, who says he belongs to Mr. Sampson below New Orleans, who bought him from Mr. Bodard 3 years ago. He is about 35, 5' 10". GEORGE W. GANT, Sheriff.

15 Sep 1841. Ran away from me 11th inst. the slave LUCY BROWN, about 20, a bright mulatto, with straight hair. She has attended my soda, cake and pie shop this summer. All persons are warned not to harbor said slave. WILLIAM SCOTT.

22 Sep 1841. $5 Reward. Ran away the 14th, the colored boy GEORGE, aged 26, very dark complexion and a yoke around his neck with no horus, and if not particularly observed will not be noticed, and a scar on his forehead. BRIDGET PHILLIPS.

19 Oct 1841. $10 Reward. Absconded on the 4th inst. the black boy ABRAM, about 6 feet high, heavy beard, very badly knock kneed. Apply Louisiana Bakery.

27 Oct 1841. $30 Reward. Ran away on the 25th inst. the girl DIANA or ANN. Ann is of yellow complexion or copper colored, about 18, rather likely, has been lately cupped on the back of the neck. She is quite intelligent. If the girl is returned of her own accord, she will not be punished. JOHN A. STEVENSON.

14 Nov 1841. $15 Reward will be paid for apprehension of the negro girl IRIS, alias NIASE, who absconded on the 12th. She is about 27, 5' 4", spare built, dark griffe. She is supposed to have absconded with a white man. C. GOODRICH, Gretna, La.

17 Nov 1841. $20 Reward. Will be paid for arrest of the slave NED who ran away from Davis's plantation, Barrataria, a few days since. Ned is a dark griffe, 45 years old, about 5' 11". He stammers a little. He has been engaged for several years at a wood yard near Carrollton.

20 Nov 1841. $20 Reward. Ran away on the 18th my negress CATHERINE, 14 years old, slim build, thick under lip and the mark of a burn on her right arm. She has holes in her ears. Speaks English only. G. B. MASON, Carrollton.

27 Nov 1841. Stolen from me the 26th of Sep., 2 negroes, one named JIM, a dark mulatto about 20, heavy built, a scar under one eye, and EBON, a black, about 18, 5' 6". I will pay $400 for their return to me. J. W. FAITH, St. Stephens, Ala. When last heard from the boys were on their way to Texas.

3 Dec 1841. Ran away from me on Saturday, an old negro woman named MARY. A liberal reward will be paid to whoever delivers her to me. JAMES M. BERRY.

4 Dec 1841. $500 Reward. Was stolen from my plantation at the mouth of Manchac, Iberville, La., the boy WRIGHT, IKE or ISAAC. He is from 12 to 15 years old, entirely black, handsome form and face, a pleasant countenance, smiles when spoken to. Disappeared on 10 November last. His skin and hands are smooth and tender, as he was a house servant. J. N. BROWN.

7 Dec 1841. $5 Reward. Ran away on 23d Nov the negro boy OSCAR DUNN, apprentice to the plastering trade. He is of griff color, about 21, 5' 10".

7 Dec 1841. $20 Reward. My servant, BEVERLY, has been missing since yesterday. He is of yellowish complexion, about 22. H. W. HOLLOWAY, Louisville, Ky.

7 Dec 1841. $20 Reward will be paid for delivery of the slave ROBERT, a mulatto about 5 feet tall, about 34. He may be concealed by his wife Betsey, my former servant, who is now the property of Mrs. Lucy Caldwell. JOHN B. BYRNE.

8 Dec 1841. $20 Reward will be paid for delivery of the bright mulatto boy ALFRED, who absconded yesterday. He is 5' 6", a house carpenter by trade.

9 Dec 1841. $10 Reward will be given for apprehension of the negress DAPNE, who absconded on Tuesday, 7th inst. She is about 35. Dapne's husband's name is Daniel who belongs to the Draining Company. Apply this newspaper.

11 Dec 1841. $20 Reward. Will be paid for the boy CHARLES, who ran away from the Maison de Sante. Charles is about 5' 5", thick set, full face, about 25; speaks French, English and Spanish. He reads quite well and attempts to pass for a free negro. Apply at the hospital.

15 Dec 1841. $50 Reward will be given to whoever will deliver to me the negro woman CHERINETTEA, vendor of merchandise, who ran away this month. Said slave is 28 or 30 years old, very black. She was formerly owned by Mr. Labrouche. She is about 5' 4", and speaks French, but little English. ULYSEE PEHAU.

17 Dec 1841. $20 Reward will be paid for apprehension of the slave JIM CLARKSON, a bright mulatto, about 22, with gray or light blue eyes, near 6' 2" tall, spare and well made. He speaks English only.

18 Dec 1841. $10 Reward. Ran away or stolen a small black girl between 9 and 10 years old named EMMA. She disappeared Thursday morning. W. T. DRAKE.

21 Dec 1841. To Whom It May Concern. Taken on the 14th inst. on board an outward bound ship, concealed in the longboat, a griffe man calling himself ALEX PETERSON, aged 30, about 5' 5", and saying he came from Nottingham, Va., about 4 years ago in the Telegraph. Having no free papers, I hold him as a slave until I am further satisfied he is not. B. A. BUKUP, Boarding Officer.

22 Jun 1842. $20 Reward. Absconded, the negro, ANDREW, 32, square made, about 5' 5", dark griffe color; has been an engineer. He was sold to me last week by Daniel Murphy, of Missouri. J. A. BEARD.

23 Jun 1842. $15 Reward. Ran away on the 13th last the mulatto girl LUCY, about 18 or 20. She formerly belonged to Mr. Soillard. She is of ordinary height, clear skin, rather stout. A. DESFORGES.

29 Jun 1842. I have in my possession a runaway slave named JOHN, taken at Fort Jackson, and says he belongs to Wilkins Hunt. The owner can have him by proving property and paying charges. W. B. G. TAYLOR, Balize.

2 Jul 1842. $10 Reward. Ran away the 16th of June a negro woman named PHERE, about 45, stout made, perfectly black, about 5' 10". The above reward will be paid to whoever will deliver her at the guard house in Mobile, near the Creek, opposite the residence of Joseph Kress.

2 Jul 1842. $20 Reward. Ran away on the 11th of June the slave SAM, a mulatto, about 25, stout built, about 6' high. His left leg is thicker than the other. DAVID BARBOUR.

4 Jul 1842. $20 Reward. Left my house on 6 June, the boy JIM COOS, a native of Havana, Cuba, a cabinet wokman by trade. He has worked in Pensacola, Mobile and Tuscaloosa, at the carpenter's business. He has worked at my residence in Perry county, Alabama for the last 2 or 3 years. He is about 50, 150 pounds, copper colored, a scar produced by a knife on his neck. He can read a little. He was employed by Robert Howtell and left my plantation returning from a visit to his wife in Marengo county, Alabama. BRITTON J. POPE.

6 Jul 1842. $10 Reward. Ran away the 20th of June, a mulatto woman named ELIZA, about 5' high, light complexion, about 30. She was purchased from Miguel Torres of Natchez 4 months ago.

13 Jul 1842. $50 Reward. Enticed away from me on the 27th of June, a negro girl named SARAH, a bright mulatto. Supposed to be taken off by Richard North, formerly stage driver, she is of middle size, very black, right forefinger off at the second joint. H. N. CARTER, Huntingdon, West Tennessee.

13 Jul 1842. $100 Reward. Absconded from Pass Christian the 28th ultimo, a mulattress, named MINERVA, the property of Mrs. Sarah Hanna, and a servant in the family of Edward Yorke. She is about 20, hair long and curly. JAMES J. HANNA.

15 Jul 1842. Ran away on the 25th of June the following slaves: DAVID, a light black, 24, 5' 5", round face. MOSES, a black, 20, 5' 10", with large underlip. Said slaves came from Virginia. JAMES REED, Plaquemines Parish.

20 Jul 1842. Were brought to the police jail of the city of Lafayette, the following slaves. A black boy about 22, calling himself AUGUSTE; says he belongs to Mr. Valdice Vermion of St. James Parish. A black boy calling himself STERLING, about 22; says he belongs to Mrs. Sally White of Wilkinson Co., Miss. A black man calling himself HARDY, about 38; says he belongs to Mr. Blanchard of New Orleans. A black boy calling himself TOM, about 20; says he belongs to Mr. Gregory of Point Coupee. A negro girl calling herself CELESTE; says she belongs to Mr. Penchon of New Orleans. M. P. JONES, Capt. of the Watch.

22 Jul 1842. $50 Reward. Ran away from the plantation of William Lile, in Claiborne Co., Miss., the negroes MOSES and JACK. Moses is about 6', dark complexion, about 21; has a gun-shot mark on his back; was purchased on 29 June from Col. Rutherford. Jack is about 5', very black, has the end of

his nose bit off and whip marks on his back. He is about 30. HOPKINS & NUGENT.

6 Aug 1842. $25 Reward. Will be paid for apprehension of the negro slave DALGER, a dark mulatto about 20, speaks French better than English, calls himself a doctor and practices among the negroes.

6 Aug 1842. $20 Reward. Ran away the 5th inst. from the residence of JAMES R. STERRETT, his negro boy ALBERT. He is about 5' 9", 23, well formed.

6 Aug 1842. $25 Reward. Ran away from her mistress on the 1st instant, the light mulatto LOUISA. She speaks French and English. She is of ordinary height, slim build, 28 years old. She waited a long time on the family of Mr. Amelung of this city.

16 Aug 1842. Ran away on the 28th of April last, JIM, 5' 8", very black, 28 years old, and FRANK, about 6' 3", yellow complexion. A liberal reward will be paid to whoever will deliver them to me at Rose Hill, Amite Co., Miss. JAMES BROWN Senr.

20 Aug 1842. $10 Reward. Ran away on the 20th of July, PHILLIS, a mulatto about 28; she has lost her upper front teeth, and is much pitted by the smallpox. D. N. STANSBURY.

26 Aug 1842. $50 Reward. Ran away from William Johnson, Circus St., a negro girl named EMELINE. She speaks French and English, is tall and slim, with long small features. She ran away with one Charles O'Neil (a sailor by profession and a white man) on Friday 19th of August, in some steamboat.

1 Sep 1842. $20 Reward. Ran away from the steamer Sultana the mulatto boy TOM HARVEY, about 20, 5' 10"; has been employed on steamboats for several years. JOHN E. HYDE.

8 Sep 1842. $15 Reward. Absconded, the negro girl MARY, property of Mary J. Hosmer. She is about 21, of dark griffe color, 5' 5" tall.

14 Sep 1842. $10 Reward. Ran away a month ago, the negro boy JOHN BULL or JOHN SMART, of low stature, stout made, 25 years old. Has a scar on his throat and is pitted by the smallpox. WILLIAM J. MILLER.

27 Sep 1842. $20 Reward. Ran away from me the 4th, 2 negro men: WASHINGTON, 5' 11", stout built, has scars on each of his hands, about 30 years old. Says he was raised in Florida and pretends to be a cook. He may claim James Thompson of Kentucky as his master. JOHN, 5' 6", common size, black, says he is a carpenter by trade and raised in South Carolina. He wears rings on his fingers. He may say he belongs to Major Shavall. S. B. STUTSON, Natchez, Miss.

29 Sep 1842. $25 reward will be paid for delivery in jail of the mulatto man named ALPHEUS, property of Mrs. Sarah Hanna, about 25, 5' 6", stout built, long hair, has a scar on his left arm. He absented himself from Pass Christian on Sunday night.

30 Sep 1842. $25 reward will be paid for arrest of the negro boy PETER, property of Mrs. Sarah Hanna. He is 19 years old, 5' 7", has long hair, a good deal of red in his cheeks, a little stoop-shouldered. He absented himself from Pass Christian Monday night.

6 Oct 1842. $10 Reward. Ran away from her home yesterday the mulattress KITTY. Had with her, her 2 children, one at the breast, and TOM, both nearly white. She was formerly owned by Mr. Merryfield.

6 Oct 1842. $20 Reward. Will be paid for delivery of the negro slave GEORGE, who ran away from the steamer Brilliant 10 days ago. He is about 25, black. He was a fireman on the Brilliant and may try to get employment on other boats. JESSE HART.

7 Oct 1842. Ran away the griffe boy, JIM, 5' 5", 26, an intelligent and shrewd fellow. E. W. SEWELL.

8 Oct 1842. $30 Reward. Ran away on the 15th of last month a bright griffe boy named ARCHY, about 20, square built. He was bought in May last. JOHN DAVID ROGERS.

9 Oct 1842. Ran away from the plantation of Alex Humphrey in St. James parish, a slave named SQUIRE, about 40, 5' 3", light complexion, has a large scar on his left breast. Speaks French and English and is very intelligent. JOSEPH A. SPROULE.

9 Oct 1842. $10 Reward for apprehension of a griffe woman named ELIZA who ran away from her master a fortnight ago. She has a crook on her left leg, small feet and large breasts. JOSE BARBRE, Gretna, La.

11 Oct 1842. $25 Reward. Will be paid for delivery of a negro named DIEGO, a bright negro, about 35, about 5' 11", speaks French, Spanish and English, very intelligent. He wore gold earrings, and has assumed the name, John Baptist. JOSEPH UZEE.

11 Oct 1842. $10 Reward. Ran away the negro man HENRY, about 23, 5' 8", very black. He speaks French and English; was bought last month from the estate of William Hall. M. CRUZAT.

14 Oct 1842. $50 in Specie!!! Will be paid to whosoever will stop the negro woman ROSINE, about 45, speaks French and English. She has a scar on her stomach, is of light complexion, common size. She has been absent about 7 months. V. DUPLESSIS.

18 Oct 1842. $10 Reward. Ran away about the 8th instant the mulatto boy JOHN, alias PETER, about 25, has a scar on his chin, upper front teeth missing, rather bowlegged. He has a wife belonging to Mr. Trigaut. ORRAN BYRD.

30 Oct 1842. $20 Reward. Absconded from me in New Orleans the 8th, the mulatto girl CHARLOTTE, about 22, 5' high, speaks French and English, and can, I believe, read and write. ADOLPHE LAYET.

30 Oct 1842. $40 reward will be paid for the delivery to Capt. Mayo, Bayou Courtableau, of the negroes HANNIBAL WILLIAMS and JOHN DUGAS, belonging to the State of Louisiana. They ran away from Bayou de Glaize.

30 Oct 1842. $40 reward will be paid for delivery of the boy WILSON, belonging to the State of Louisiana. He is about 5' 8", of a bright mulatto color. He was purchased of J. F. MILLER.

9 Nov 1842. $10 Reward will be paid for delivery of the black man BERRY, about 40, 5' 8", stout built, a blemish on his right eye.

12 Nov 1842. $20 Reward. Ran away a negro man named ALBERT, 22, black complexion, 2 lower front teeth out. Two fingers on his left hand are stiff. He is supposed to have absconded with 3 white men who broke jail in Concordia on the 3d instant. JAMES A. TUCKER, Vidalia, La.

20 Nov 1842. $20 Reward. Ran away the negress MARY ANN, near 6 feet high. She has a husband named Jack, belonging to Mr. Woods.

22 Nov 1842. $15 Reward will be paid for the negro man STEPHEN, a tall stout fellow marked with smallpox. Has been a drayman for several years.

27 Nov 1842. $10 Reward. Absconded 14 days ago a mulatto man named WILLIAM FOSTER, alias Stuttering Bill, of genteel deportment. He is well known as a steamboat steward. D. FLEISCHMANN.

30 Nov 1842. $10 Reward for my slave HARRIETT, who absconded the 18th instant. She is about 26, 5 feet high, of mulatto tinge. She speaks French and English. She is in the third month of pregnancy. She took with her, her mulatto child, aged 14 months, with very long hair. JOE VIGO.

3 Dec 1842. $25 Reward. Left on the 28th ultimo, the griff boy CYRUS, about 28, spare made, about 5' 7". LEONARD HESS.

4 Dec 1842. $25 Reward for delivery to me of my negro woman MARIA. She absconded 6 weeks ago. She is about 40, of dark complexion, middle size. The middle fingers of her right hand are grown together. She speaks French and English. SAMUEL BELL.

7 Dec 1842. $10 Reward. Ran away a negro boy, ANTHONY, about 23, 5' 6", slender make.

15 Dec 1842. $20 Reward. Ran away yesterday the slave MARIA, a dark mulatto about 17, stout built, about 5' 5".

16 Dec 1842. Ran away from the residence of Thomas T. Davis, near Kingston, on the 19th of August, a negro man belonging to me, named EDMUND, sometimes called HENRY, 23, 5' 9"; has a scar across his nose and forehead, one front tooth out. He formerly was owned by Mr. Hawkins of Tennessee, and latterly by Mr. James of New Orleans, and Mr. Soria of Natchez. JOHN S. JONES, Natchez, Miss.

12 Jan 1843. $20 Reward. Ran away on the 1st instant the slave ELIZA, about 20, dark griffe, slender, about 5' 6", front teeth rather wide apart. Was employed by Mrs. Hanna on Canal st. JACOB BEN.

13 Jan 1843. $20 reward will be paid for apprehension and delivery to us of our negro boy WILSON, a griffe, 5' 4", tall head of hair, a scar on his upper lip, speaks French and English. BOWE & CRENSHAW.

20 Jan 1843. $200 Reward! Stop the villains. On the night of the 9th instant my shuck pen was set on fire, a trunk in my house was robbed of 173 dollars in specie, and 4 of my negroes stolen. The negroes are named--DAVE, 18 or 19, tall, black. JORDON, black, with a scar on one thigh. MARIAH, 9, black. BETSY, 7 or 8, black, smart and active. WILLIAM JARRELL, Jackson, Butts Co., Ga.

24 Jan 1843. $25 reward. Ran away on the 23d instant the slave NANCY, about 34, a dark mulattress, 5' 3".

28 Jan 1843. $10 reward will be paid for delivery to me of the negro boy MOSES, about 5' 7", 23 years old. He has one scar under his left breast, one on his right cheek, and one on his left hand. WILLIAM J. ANDERSON, New Basin.

14 Feb 1843. $10 Reward. Will be paid for recovery of the negro boy CORNELIUS, stolen from me on Thursday. Has a scar on one cheek, has lost some of his front teeth. P. FLYNN.

14 Feb 1843. $25 Reward. Ran away the 5th inst. the griff man TOM, about 30, 5' 11". He has been a fireman on steamboats, and has worked on board ships. T. HAGGETT.

15 Feb 1843. $10 Reward. Ran away on 27 January, a mulatto man named WILLIAM, about 20, a Creole of this place, 5' 7". He formerly belonged to S. Gaunault, who sold him to C. Lamarque. He has a wife in Esplanade st.

15 Feb 1843. $10 Reward will be given for the negro boy HAL, who ran off from the steamer Swan on the 4th instant. He is about 20, and very black. He was purchased from Mr. Zuntz of Mobile.

15 Feb 1843. $10 Reward. Ran away the 1st, the slave griffe woman CAROLINE, 35, 5' 4", speaks French and little English. She took with her, her mulatto child CORINNE, about 6, who speaks English. J. B. WALTON.

25 Feb 1843. $5 reward for a negress called ELIZA, about 10 years old, who absented herself 10 days since. She is good looking and speaks French and English. ISABELLA COX.

1 Mar 1843. Ran away a negro man named PRIMAS, formerly owned by A. Sidney Robinson. He is from 30 to 35, 5' 9",

square made, of brown copper complexion. PETER DOYLE, Mobile.

5 Mar 1843. $20 Reward. Ran away from me at Barbour Co., Ala., on 22nd October of 1842, a mulatto boy named FOUNTAIN, 30 to 35, slender form, very intelligent. He has marks of lashings on his back. ISHAM JOHNSON, Irwinton, Ala.

7 Mar 1843. Strayed off, on the 1st inst. a dark colored negro boy named TONEY, aged 10 or 11.

9 Mar 1843. $25 Reward. Left the subscriber on March 5th a negro man named WILLIAM, formerly owned by Clinton & Port Hudson Railroad Company. He is from 25 to 30, 5' 6", of copper complexion, speaks English only. J. DRUMMOND.

14 Mar 1843. Ran away yesterday a negro man named ANTHONY, yellow complexion, 24 or 25, 5' 7". A liberal reward will be paid to whoever will deliver him to me at 179 Gravier st. DAVID MIDDLETON.

18 Mar 1843. Was committed to the jail of Madison Co., Miss., on the 5th of February, by James Priestly, a negro boy named JANUARY, about 24, 5' 7". He says he belongs to Mr. Blanchard of New Orleans and that he made his escape at the mouth of the Red River, from a steamboat carrying him upriver to a plantation of said Blanchard. S. HAMBLEN, Sheriff, Canton, Miss.

19 Mar 1843. $20 Reward. Absconded last evening a mulatto boy named ARTHUR PERKINS, about 35, 5' 9", speaks only English.

24 Mar 1843. $10 Reward. The boy THOMAS, about 18 or 20, absconded this morning from the steamboat Ellen

Kirkman. He is about 5' 8", very dark complexion, quite intelligent. I recently purchased him from William Harris, of Jackson, Miss. MILES GAMBLINZ.

30 Mar 1843. $10 Reward. Left the New Orleans Cotton Press 10 days ago the mulatto boy HENRY BURNS, aged 30, low stature, thick set. BEHAN & MITCHELL.

2 Apr 1843. $100 Reward will be paid for apprehension of the slave HANNAH, a likely, slender girl 18 years old, 5 feet high, quite black. It is supposed she was taken away by one Alexander Black, overseer for Jesse Cowan for the last 3 years.

4 Apr 1843. $5 reward will be given for the mulatto boy BILL, who left me the 3d instant. He is about 14, of very light color, straight hair, has a wart on the outside of his small fingers. J. H. HOWARD.

12 Apr 1843. $20 Reward. Will be paid for delivery of the black boy CELESTE, a creole of this city. Speaks French and English, is about 5' 3" and is bowlegged. R. F. NICHOLS.

18 Apr 1843. $5 reward for apprehension of the boy JOHN HARDY or JOHN COYLE. He is entirely black, about 5' 10", rather good looking. He wears earrings and is very proud of his deportment. He formerly drove an ash cart in the city. JAMES COYLE.

1 Apr 1843. $25 Reward. Absconded on the 9th of February at Vicksburg, Miss., a negro boy named EDMUND. He is of copper color, stout built, about 26, 6 feet high and speaks English only. PILCHER & RAYBURN.

5 May 1843. $10 Reward. Strayed from my residence yesterday a copper colored boy named WALKER, aged 6 years, dressed in blue cottonade pants and jacket. He is supposed to have followed the soldiers away. WARREN STONE, M.D.

9 May 1843. $20 will be paid for delivery of the black boy WILLIAM, who absconded the 1st inst. He speaks French and English and is about 5' 8", and formerly belonged to Joseph Ragese, and went by the name of Grand William. Also, $20 for the black girl DELPHIE, about 5 feet tall, slender, formerly belonging to Captain Hutchins. She absconded 2 months ago.

11 May 1843. $20 Reward. Absconded the 6th inst. the mulatto boy FELIX (he calls himself FELIX PASSAGUAY). He is 26 to 28 years old, 5' 9", very fair complexion, straight black hair, speaks French and English, and can also write. He was owned in St. Louis some years ago by Mr. Chouteau, where his mother resides. He may be easily detected from a number of figures &c on his arms in India ink.

11 May 1843. $20 reward. Ran away from me on the 1st inst. the negro man SINUS, about 26, 5' 5", formerly owned by Major Digges, of this city. J. A. BEARD.

12 May 1843. $50 Reward. Ran away from me on the 7th, my negro boys, ISAAC and JIM. Isaac is 22, 6 feet tall, dark. Jim is rather yellow, 5' 6", about 30. DANIEL McLAURIN, Dry Creek, Covington Co., Miss. (It is possible the boys were decoyed off by an Irishman named John Keaffe, who has his name written on his arm.)

16 May 1843. $10 Reward. Absconded on 15 April, the mulatto woman BETSY, 5' 4", 35 to 40, upper teeth mostly

gone, formerly belonged to J. B. BYRNES on Canal St. L. A. CALDWELL.

16 May 1843. $10 Reward. Ran away yesterday the negro boy HENRY, about 14, belonging to Dr. G. C. Forsyth, at the English Turn, La. Speaks French and English.

19 May 1843. $20 Reward. Absconded from the subscriber on the 17th, the negro boy BILLY about 25, stout built, slightly bowlegged. R. T. DOWNEY.

7 Jun 1843. $20 Reward. Ran away the negro man BERRY, about 57, purchased from S. N. Hite. J. A. BEARD.

8 Jun 1843. $5 Reward. Ran away in February a negro woman named BARBARA, about 50, quite tall and very black. ANTHONY BILHARTZ, Lafayette, La.

9 Jun 1843. $20 Reward. Ran away from me on 20th April 2 negro girls, CAROLINE, about 20, and CLARA, about 14. Caroline was purchased of Mr. Slatter; Clara of Mr. Campbell. Clara has a scar on her upper lip. JAMES TYSON, Balize.

13 Jun 1843. $10 Reward. Will be paid for the negro man STEPHEN, a tall, stout fellow, pitted by smallpox, a drayman in the city for the past 5 years. CHARLES A. JACOBS.

13 Jun 1843. $20 Reward. Ran away, the negro boy SIMS, 26, 5' 5", and formerly owned by Major Digges of this city. J. A. BEARD.

15 Jun 1843. $10 Reward. Ran away day before yesterday, 2 negro boys SIMON and HORACE, who have belonged to me for the past 4 years. Sims is a griffe, 12 or 14. Horace is about the same age. L. A. CALDWELL.

1 Jul 1843. Ran away from me near Clinton, La., the 13th of June, the following negroes: SAM, about 26, of copper color, 5' 10". VARDEMAN, of copper color, 5' 6". These 2 negroes were purchased from D. Middleton in New Orleans on May 2, and came from Kentucky. HARRY, about 24, very black color. He was bought from H. F. Peterson of New Orleans in May. HENRY JACKSON, sometimes called "General," about 24, 5' 9", very black. His right leg is shorter than the left. A. D. PALMER.

4 Jul 1843. $10 Reward. Ran away almost 10 days ago, the well known boy, REUBEN, about 50, 5' 4". W. A. PECK.

13 Jul 1843. $10 Reward. Absented himself from my residence at Greenville, the boy JACK, a griffe, about 22, 5' 5", somewhat bowlegged. Speaks French and English. He formerly belonged to Samuel J. Peters. JOHN GREENE.

14 Jul 1843. $40 reward to whoever will arrest 2 negro men who absconded from the plantation of Henry Dayal, Mount Houmas, Ascension Parish the 9th instant. FOUNTAIN, about 45, stout and square built, and HENRY, 35, middle size. Fountain was purchased last year from Mark Davis; Henry from Mr. Rutherford. P. ROTCHFORD.

20 Jul 1843. $10 Reward for the mulatto boy AUGUSTE, who ran away the 16th inst. He is about 17, speaks French and English, stands about 5' 5", has a scar across one eye. J. A. BEARD.

20 Jul 1843. $10 Reward. Ran away on Friday the negro woman LOUISE, or LUCINDA; 26, speaks French and English, ordinary height, well known as a Bouquet Marchande.

20 Jul 1843. $10 Reward. Absented himself on the 18th inst. CARTER, a mulatto boy, about 23, 5' 6". BENJAMIN KENDIG.

25 Jul 1843. $10 Reward will be paid for arrest of the black boy LONDON, who absconded from the steamboat Yazoo on the 9th. He has a scar on his face, and is about 5' 4" tall. HAINES & CO.

27 Jul 1843. $10 Reward for apprehension of the negro woman MERANTHE, who ran away from P. E. LAYET's residence in Robin St. She speaks French, English and Spanish. She is 5 feet high.

28 Jul 1843. $10 Reward will be paid for the slave ELLIS, 45, 5' 8 or 9", square built; has worked the last 7 months at the Louisiana Cotton Press. P. SHEILS.

28 Jul 1843. $5 Reward. Ran away from me on the 20th, the girl ANN or DIANA, a mulatress, about 18, 5' 4". JOHN A. STEVENSON.

28 Jul 1843. $10 Reward will be paid for the black girl HARRIET, who absconded on July 25. She is 5' 3", about 26, speaks English and French. JOSEPH UREE.

1 Aug 1843. $15 Reward. Ran away the slave SALLY or MARIA, a dark griffe, 22, 4' 10", upper teeth much decayed. She speaks French and English. She formerly belonged to Mr. Tricou of Carrollton. It is said her mother lives down the coast. T. WOLFE.

6 Aug 1843. $300 Reward. Whereas I have heard that my boy MOSES, who ran away about 5 months ago, has been seen in Liverpool (England) by Mr. Rogers of the ship Cairo, I will

pay above reward for information leading to the conviction of those who decoyed him away. Moses requested Mr. Rogers to present his compliments to me and say he was in Liverpool. CHARLES WHITE.

17 Aug 1843. $15 Reward. Ran away 5 weeks ago, the girl FANNY, 21, stout built, round face, speaks French and English, 4' 8" tall, belonging to Mr. Baptiste Roussel.

23 Aug 1843. $10 Reward. Will be paid for delivery of the black girl DELPHI, about 35, tall, thin, and rough spoken. She formerly belonged to Capt. Hutchins. She absconded the 6th inst. JAMES PHILLIPS.

30 Aug 1843. $10 reward will be paid for delivery of the negro boy LOUIS, a dark griffe, 20, about 5' 4", with a bunch of hair on his chin. He left my house last night. HENRY FERRIS.

5 Sep 1843. $15 reward will be paid for apprehension of the mulatto boy EMERSON. He absconded on 27 August from Pass Christian. He is about 5' 4", wore a mustache and has a pleasant countenance. E. L. TRACY.

10 Sep 1843. To owners of cotton presses, tobacco warehouses, and bricklayers--take notice that my mulatto boy GEORGE, about 27, has not been near me for upwards of 2 months. He is slim, about 5' 6", dark complexion, has a small round face. He is well known by the bricklayers of this city. A liberal reward will be given to whoever brings him to his master, ANTHONY FERNANDEZ.

1 Oct 1843. $5 reward will be paid for my mulatto boy CLEMIRE, but sometimes calls himself EMILLE. He left my residence 27th September. He is good looking, middle size,

with black curly hair, about 19, and speaks French and English. SILPHIDE PERDEAUX.

4 Oct 1843. $10 Reward. Ran away from the undersigned the slave AGNES, about 26, low stature, stoutly made, black color, speaks French and English. Had an iron collar around her neck when she left. VIRG. LEVACHEZ.

12 Oct 1843. $100 Reward. Stolen from the subscriber 29 Sep. a negro woman called LETTY, about 30, of chocolate color, with crooked fingers. I will pay above reward for delivery of the slave and thief to me. JAMES H. MARTIN, Mobile.

22 Oct 1843. $10 reward for apprehension of the colored man NEEDHAM, 24, 5' 10", well made and fine looking. Had on large heavy whiskers. He is well known on steamboats, having been on board the Desoto, the Star and others. Officers of steamboats are particularly requested not to employ him. WILLIAM PARKER.

25 Oct 1843. $20 Reward. Ran away the negro man JOHN, about 35, black color, stout made, one leg shorter than the other and rather crooked. He has been employed on steamboats as cook and may pass himself off in that capacity. JOHN H. RAHDERS.

31 Oct 1843. $20 Reward. Ran away 29th inst. a griffe woman named NANCY, about 26, very stout, 5' 4". About a year ago she was hired at the National Hotel, and afterwards for 2 months at the Mint.

31 Oct 1843. $20 Reward. Ran away a negro girl named ROSANNA, about 20, 5' 4", dark complexion, large lips.

1 Nov 1843. $25 Reward. Ran away the 24th ultimo, a colored boy named WILLIAM, 25 or 30, 5' 5", straight black hair, might be mistaken for a Mexican. When last seen he wore an "Imperial." He was formerly the property of the late T. Kennedy, and is a painter by trade.

22 Nov 1843. $20 Reward. Ran away the 18th inst. from his mistress, 53 Bourbon st. the negro boy VICTOR, about 17, speaks French and a little English.

28 Nov 1843. $10 Reward will be paid for information that will return to her mistress the woman NANCY, who has been missing since the 10th instant. Mrs. LAYTON.

28 Nov 1843. $10 Reward. To any person who will arrest my negro SAM, 25, 5' 6", front teeth decayed, about 140 pounds. JAMES D. TODD.

28 Nov. 1843. $50 Reward. Ran away on the 10th inst. the mulatto boy known as JIM ALONG JOSEY, 14, ordinary size, known to be a great dancer. F. H. HATCH.

6 Dec 1843. $100 Reward. For the negro woman CASSEY or CATHERINE, well known in the city, as having for a long time belonged to Mr. Cantrell, St. James Parish, and afterwards to Mlle. Belle, in New Orleans. She is about 40 to 45 years old, has no upper front teeth. P. REYNARD.

14 Dec 1843. $25 Reward. Ran away 2 months ago a negro boy named LEE, 4' 8", of a red color, marked by the smallpox. I suppose he was enticed away by two white men in a skiff. JOSEPH COLLETT, Bayou Grand Callion, 12 miles below Houma, Terrebonne parish.

15 Dec 1843. Reward for NANCY, about 21, rather short and fleshy and quite black. Has been seen about the city in company of Harrison, a slave who works at brick laying and plastering. A suitable reward will be paid for her apprehension. H. A. HUNTINGTON.

28 Dec 1843. $20 Reward. Absconded from the subscriber's plantation in Jefferson Parish last September, the slave RICHARD, 35, 5' 4", with prominent cheek bones--speaks French and English. Also, $20 reward for the boy CLINTON, a runaway from the same place since last August. He is about 30, with a scar on one of his legs caused by a burn. Speaks English only. LUCIAN LABRANCHE.

29 Dec 1843. Ran away yesterday a negro girl named ROXANA, about 29, dark complexion, below middle size and well formed. Whoever arrests her and gives information at the office of the Picayune will receive the above reward.

12 Jan 1844. $50 Reward. Ran away the 8th instant, the negro boy PHILIP, about 30, 5' 8", light complexion, a scar on his upper lip, and bald on top of his head. U. BOULIGNY, JR.

12 Jan 1844. $10 Reward. Ran away last Friday, my black boy JOHN, who sometimes calls himself PHIL. He is about 30, and formerly belonged to Mr. Mendelin Doli. JAMES PHILLIPS.

19 Jan 1844. $10 Reward. Absconded a black man JIM, a carpenter by trade, of common size, good form and address, full face, very fine set of teeth. May wear a long beard on his chin. D. FLEISCHMAN.

26 Jan 1844. $50 Reward. Ran away on Sunday a negro man named NED, or EDMUND, 23, 6' high, light complexion, a

scar on one of his arms, weighs about 185 pounds. He was once in the chain gang of this city as a runaway, and worked 2 years at the Cotton Press. LEWIS HYNOR.

26 Jan 1844. $50 Reward will be paid on conviction of the person found harboring my servant girl MORNA, or $10 for her delivery in jail. Morna is about 17, 5' 2", light copper color, acquiline nose. GEORGE A. BEARD.

7 Feb 1844. $5 Reward. Ran away a black boy, JIM, 5', a scar on his lip, caused by the kick of a horse. He speaks French, English and Spanish. FRANCIS GONZALEZ.

10 Feb 1844. $10 Reward. Will be paid for delivery of NELSON, who absconded on the 7th inst. He is about 30, 5' 7", heavy made, stout, and broad shouldered. He speaks very slow and answers very sullenly. He can read and write. E. P. SHAW.

11 Feb 1844. $15 Reward. Ran away 2 weeks since, my slave girl ELIZA, about 12 years old, small and a negro; she is very good looking and very artful. J. FOX.

17 Feb 1844. $15 Reward. Absconded on the 15th inst. a mulatto woman, RACHEL, about 40, had on an iron collar with 3 prongs, with a small bell attached to each prong. It is supposed she will attempt to get to Franfort, Ky. J. F. BUFFET.

22 Feb 1844. $10 Reward. Ran away on the 11th inst. a negro boy named PETER, 22 years old. He is middle size, has high cheek bones, very large white eyes, and a rather sullen appearance. Mrs. KERR.

28 Feb 1844. $5 Reward. Absconded this morning, the negro man, lately owned by Mr. Mix, about 40, 6' 6" high, going by the names of ISAM and ISAK. He is a cook and has been on steamboats. H. WEIL.

29 Feb 1844. $10 Reward. Absented herself on the 23d inst. the negro woman NANCY, about 5 feet high, stout, thick set, black complexion and good countenance. She is about 40 years old. She arrived from Charleston, S. C., last December in the brig Powhattan. The above reward will be paid for her delivery to any city jail. WILLIS HOLMES.

2 Mar 1844. $10 Reward. Absconded Sunday evening the negress JANE, about 19, stout made, short in height, and rather talkative.

5 Mar 1844. $20 Reward. Ran away from me on the 2d inst. my mulatto slave BETSY, formerly belonging to J. B. Byrne. She is about 5' 2" tall, has bad front teeth, high cheek bones, and is about 35 years old. B. P. DRAKE, her master.

9 Mar 1844. $10 Reward. Absconded on the 6th inst. the negro girl NANCY, about 50, speaks French and English; has no front teeth, very dark skin. She took with her, her daughter, a mulatto, aged about 7 years. She also has a daughter on Girod St. J. A. BRAUD.

14 Mar 1844. $5 Reward. Ran away on the 4th inst. the negro girl HARRIET JANE, about 14 or 15, stout and thick set, good teeth. HUGH McCLORY.

20 Mar 1844. $25 Reward. The boy HUMPHREY left his home on the 2d inst. He is of dark yellow color, stout built, about 20, and is a barber by trade. He is about 5' 4" tall. R. F. NICHOLS.

21 Mar 1844. $10 Reward. Ran away the 12th inst. 2 negroes, a man and a woman. The man is named ABRAM and commonly known as ABRAM INSKO, about 25, 6' high, high forehead, black, front teeth out or defective. (Name of woman not mentioned). H. J. DURKER.

27 Mar 1844. $20 Reward. Ran away from 231 Canal St. a few days since, a yellow woman named CHARLOTTE, of ordinary size, from 20 to 25, has a slight scar on one cheek, and bad teeth. She has a very erect walk. A. D. WOOLDRIDGE.

29 Mar 1844. $50 Reward. Ran away on the 27th, a negro girl named ELIZA, about 14, black complexion, rather slim form, handsome face, upper teeth somewhat decayed. RICHARD KING.

3 Apr 1844. $10 reward will be paid for delivery of the boy CHARLES; he formerly belonged to Mr. Conlin of this city, and was supposed to have left Mobile on the steamboat John L. Day on Saturday last. J. A. BEARD.

4 Apr 1844. $100 Reward will be paid to whoever will return to me the griff, WILSON, who ran away on 10 July last. He is of short stature, delicate figure, about 24 years old. He has been a marchand at the market house of the 1st Municipality. A. ROBELOT.

9 Apr 1844. $10 Reward will be given for apprehension of the negro man WASHINGTON, who absconded from the Union Cotton Press on the 28th ultimo. He is about 5' 6", 28 years old, very black, has large eyes, thick lips and an intelligent face.

10 Apr 1844. $20 Reward. Ran away on the 23d ultimo the servant girl SARAH ANN, aged about 18, small stature, griffe colored, speaks rapidly. A suitable reward will be paid for her apprehension. THOMAS O. MEUX.

10 Apr 1844. $5 Reward. Ran away a negro woman named LUCY, property of the subscriber. She is black, has a stiff finger on her right hand. Whoever will bring her to me at Circus and Julia streets will receive above reward. CHARLES MEYER.

11 Apr 1844. $10 Reward. Absconded, the griff man BURREL, aged 40 years. Said slave is well known on the river as a cook and steward. He has long hair, is of short stature, and bowlegged. He belongs to Mr. Cuthbert Buillit of this city.

19 Apr 1844. $10 Reward. Ran away from my house on the 17th inst. the negro ROBERT, alias BOS, 18, 5' 8", speaks French and English. He has a reddish complexion. He is a cigar maker. JOHN N. GLAUDIN.

23 Apr 1844. $10 Reward. Will be paid for apprehension and delivery of the negro woman ELIZA, who absconded on Thursday last. She is about 27, 5' 3", very dark complexion. J. W. WOODLAND.

26 Apr 1844. $10 Reward. Ran away yesterday the yellow girl MARY ANN, about 30, 5' 2", large mouth, thick lips, rather forbidding countenance, very black eyes and nearly straight hair. She speaks only English. E. BLANC.

2 May 1844. $15 Reward. Ran away 18th March the negro boy PETER, of brown complexion, about 20, speaks French and English; about 5' 7", slender build, knock-kneed, hair short and curly. HUGH BELL.

2 May 1844. $10 Reward for my griffe girl MARY ANN, formerly the property of Col. J. W. Lane, 5' 4", 22 years old. R. A. KENT.

3 May 1844. $20 Reward. My black boy GRIFFIN absconded. He may try to get up the river. He is 22, 5' 4", has large eyes. His looks are quick and uneasy. ANTHONY FERNANDEZ.

14 May 1844. $20 Reward. Ran away Saturday a middle aged black woman named MIMA. She is about 5' 5", has large features and a very gruff manner. WILLIAM HENDERSON.

14 May 1844. $5 Reward. Ran away Monday evening a griffe girl named MARTHA, belonging to Charles Allen. She is blind of her right eye and generally wears a handkerchief over it.

24 May 1844. $20 Reward. Ran away 20 May a negro girl named REBECCA, alias VICTORIA. She is of light color, about 23, well formed, common height.

5 Jun 1844. $10 Reward. Absconded on 23 May, a negro man named CHARLES, very black, about 25. He professes to be a painter. Mrs. ANN ROSENDALE.

9 Jun 1844. $50 Reward for the yellow boy JOHN HUNTER, who absconded the 19th of May. He is about 20, 5' 5", has some marks of the whip on the back of his neck, is very intelligent. H. F. WADE.

9 Jun 1844. Left the subscriber residing near Clinton, La., on the 12th of March, a negro man about 27, by the name of ALFRED, often called BOGS--about 5' 9 or 10", light copper color. He is something of a carpenter. A. D. PALMER.

7 Jul 1844. $20 Reward for the negro woman HANNAH, about 45; she absented herself from my dwelling last February. She is of low stature and is inclined to be fat. W. M. LAMBETH.

7 Jul 1844. Was committed to the jail of West Feliciana, La., the slave ELIZA, who says she belongs to James Williams of New Orleans. She is about 8 or 9 years old, of light copper complexion and about 4' tall. The owner is requested to take her out of jail. JOHN H. HAND, Deputy Sheriff.

11 Jul 1844. $150 Reward. Absconded from my premises near Raceville, Hancock Co., Miss., on the 18th ultimo, my slave PETER, about 28, 5' 5", copper complexion, high cheek bones, high forehead, square shouldered, stout made, and very active. He plays well on the violin and is a very sensible fellow. His mother and brother, who are free, reside in New Orleans. DAVID R. WINGATE, Raceville, Miss.

12 Jul 1844. $10 Reward. Ran away from the schooner Cornelia the 1st, the negro boy RICHARD or BIG DICK, about 30, 6 feet high, speaks English and a little French. He is strong and well made, has a large mouth and thick lips. R. PHILLIPS.

21 Jul 1844. $25 Reward. Absconded the mulatto woman named HARRIETT, about 35, 5' 8", with her son CASSIMER, a mulatto about 14 years old. WILLIAM BELL.

25 Jul 1844. $100 Reward. Ran away 28 June, a bright mulatto boy named BILL, about 25, straight black hair, of genteel appearance, looks more like a Mexican than a negro. ISABEL M. HUTTON.

25 Jul 1844. $10 Reward. Ran away a bright mulatto girl named LOUISA, about 23, stout made, speaks English only. She was raised at Josiah Gray's plantation near Bayou Sara. RICHARD POCHELU.

1 Aug 1844. $15 reward will be paid for delivery to me of the woman FANNY, 34 or 40, 5 feet high, with eyes of a reddish complexion, produced by drinking. She formerly belonged to Mr. Randolph. J. A. BEARD.

3 Aug 1844. $25 Reward. Ran away in June, 1843, the black woman MARY, 40, ordinary size, coarse features, speaks English only. She has very bad teeth. She is from Paris, Kentucky. H. DUFILHO.

3 Aug 1844. $10 Reward. Ran away yesterday a negro boy, JOE, who formerly belonged to Mr. William Prehn. Joe is very black, 18 or 19 years old.

9 Aug 1844. $10 Reward. Ran away last evening the negress CHARLOTTE, about 15 years old, has a scar on her neck from a burn. She speaks French and English. G. W. GEORGE.

13 Aug 1844. Ran away from the subscriber, living in Barbour Co., Ala., near Eufala, 15 June last, a negro fellow named GEORGE, about 30, low and thick set, quick spoken, and inclined to be yellow. He may try to make his way West, somewhere near Texas, as his wife was lately removed to that section by John Currie. A liberal reward will be paid for his return to me. ROBERT MARTIN, Near Eufala, Ala.

15 Aug 1844. $10 Reward. Ran away 31 July a griffe girl who calls herself MARY DODSON, about 17, 5 feet high.

21 Aug 1844. $25 Reward. The boy WILLIAM WALLACE has been absent since the 18th instant. He is a dark negro, 17, 5' 9", large frame and a slouching walk. W. E. TURNER.

22 Aug 1844. $10 reward will be paid for delivery to me of the negro girl ANNETTE, aged 12 or 13 years. Has a large mouth, seldom closed. F. H. HATCH.

24 Aug 1844. $10 Reward will be paid for delivery of my boy JOHN or PHILL, a dark negro, 5' 8", stout and easy in his talk. He absconded the 19th instant. JAMES PHILLIPS.

6 Sep 1844. $20 Reward. Ran away on board the steamer J. Dupre the 18th ultimo, two slaves, ELLICK and FOSTER. Ellick is 5' 8", black, with remarkably smooth skin and crooked legs. Foster is black, 5' 5", has a sulky look, and is somewhat deaf. DAVID T. BAGLEY, Covington, La.

11 Sep 1844. Ran away on Saturday, EMILINE, a black. She has crooked fingers and a thumb without a bone on the right hand, and is about 20 years old. R. SLARK.

14 Sep 1844. Ran away from my residence the 8th inst. the following slaves: JOHN TAYLOR, griff, between 35 and 40 years old, 5' 6 or 7", a little bowlegged. JAMES ROBERTSON, a griff, 40, 5' 9", long curly hair. JOHN HARRISON, a griff, about 20, 5' 4", with good figure. FRONTIN, 12, negro, a very intelligent house servant. Also, ANDREW, a very dark negro from 30 to 35, about 5' 10". The bridge of his nose broken by the kick of a mule. $50 reward for John Taylor and James Robertson, $25 for each of the others. SAMUEL FAGOT, St. James Parish.

22 Sep 1844. $10 Reward. Ran away on the 8th inst. a likely negro girl about 20 named EMMA. T. M. WADSWORTH.

24 Sep 1844. $5 reward for arrest of the negro men NELSON and CAESAR. Nelson is stout, good looking, and black. He had been working with Mr. William Johnson, a builder. Caesar is a handsome mulatto, 5' 7", and has been working on board ships. They were bought by Thomas R. Wolfe the past summer from a Mr. or Dr. Carter. THOMAS W. SCOTT.

8 Oct 1844. Ran away from me at Griffin, Pike Co., Ga., 17 Sep. a negro man named DICK, about 30, very black, well made. He is a very good workman either as a carpenter or wagon maker. For his return to me I will pay $20. THOMAS J. JOHNSON.

8 Oct 1844. Ran away from the Union Bakery on the 5th inst. the mulatto man SAM, about 20, about 6' high, stout built. DAVID BARBOUR.

13 Oct 1844. $10 Reward. Strayed or stolen on the 9th, EDMOND, about 18, 5' 7", intelligent face, lately arrived from Missouri. L. Y. LUSK.

20 Oct 1844. Ran away from Covington, La., on 9 Sep., a negro man named PETER, about 35, 5' 3", stout made, very black. T. J. MORTEE.

26 Oct 1844. $20 will be paid for delivery of my mulatto boy WILLIAM (formerly belonging to Adolphe Plauche) aged 22, 5' 6", a little bowlegged. Speaks French, English and Spanish. Had his ears pierced and one earring in. AARON COHEN.

7 Nov 1844. $10 Reward will be paid for the mulatto boy BARTLETT, a runaway--he is 5' 6", about 26, a bread seller on Lafayette st. D'AQUIN BROTHERS.

7 Nov 1844. Ran away from the plantation of the subscriber in St. Mary parish, Attakapas, last September, the following negroes: DAVE, 45, of yellow complexion, about 5' 10", coarse bushy hair, is badly ruptured and wears a large steel truss; lively and talkative. HENRY WILSON, 30, 5' 7", has many scars on his arms and legs. ADDISON, 30, 5' 7", well made, is crippled in the left hand, has a scar on his forehead. GEORGE, 50, 6', slim made, very black, is intelligent, and reads and writes, and is very fond of playing the violin. He was sold to me by Thomas Plemings of Miller Co., Mo. BEN, about 25, 5' 7", yellow complexion, stout made; has scars on the left knee and about the ankles, proceeding from dog bites. $50 will be paid for each of the above described negroes. DANIEL P. SPARK.

9 Nov 1844. $10 Reward. Ran away from the subscriber the negro boy JEAN, lately owned by Celestine Populus, about 5' 6", 21 years old. JAMES PHILLIPS.

20 Nov 1844. $25 Reward. For a negro boy who ran away from me last summer. His name is JACK, some 6' 8" tall, 21 or 22, black complexion, slender and close set. I purchased him from G. W. Barnes of Halifax, N. C. in March. WILLIAM CAMPBELL, Kemper Co., Miss.

21 Nov 1844. $5 Reward. Ran away on the 7th inst. my negro boy DAN, about 5' 10", 28 years old, very black, abrupt in his speech, has been a drayman for some years. J. FOX.

1 Dec 1844. $10 Reward. Ran away on the 28th ultimo, the negro BEN, 5' 9", thickly set, about 35, speaks French and English. G. B. MASON, Carrollton, La.

10 Dec 1844. $10 Reward. Ran away on the 7th inst. from Fugene Forlier's plantation, 15 miles above the city, the negro

boy ALECK, 22, 5' 9", slim made, of a reddish black complexion, with straight, fine a hair. J. A. BEARD.

10 Dec 1844. $500 Reward. Will be paid for sufficient evidence to convict any person or persons taking and harboring following slaves: JIM, and SIDNEY, his wife, about 26 years old; SAM, thin-faced, a knot on his back. Said slaves left Quokib Island on the 1st inst. in a skiff near the lighthouse at Bayou St. John. Said negroes are from Georgia. ALEXANDER GEORGE, Fort Pike, La.

11 Dec 1844. $10 Reward. Ran away on 24 October the negro boy JIM, about 5' 10", griff complexion, stout built, wears rings in his ears. Formerly belonged to Daniel McAuley and works as a cooper in tobacco warehouses. RICHARD CHARLES.

13 Dec 1844. Notice--ran away from me in parish of East Baton Rouge, near Port Hudson, the following negroes: JOHN, black complexion, 5' 8 or 9", large and full eyes, 25 or 26. ANDERSON, bright yellow color, 5' 8 or 9", stout, about 24. BILL, of bright yellowish color, 5' 6 or 7", spare built, a scar on the right foot caused by an axe, 13 to 20 years old. They were lately brought from Missouri. The negro boy I bought of William H. Williams of New Orleans, last June. MABACHIA BRADFORD.

11 Dec 1844. $15 Reward. Absconded from Duparc Brothers & Locoul's plantation in St. James parish, a negro man named OSTER BREGIS, about 25, 5' 5". He is a good cooper and speaks English and a little French.

11 Dec 1844. $10 Reward. Ran away on the 4th inst. a negro woman named JUDY. She is about 5', 30 years old, quite black, pock marked, 2 upper front teeth out. She has her toes

off from both feet. Speaks French and English fluently. MARY S. TAYLOR.

14 Dec 1844. $10 reward will be paid for the mulatto girl SARAH or SALLY, who absconded the 8th instant. She is about 28, with straight hair. SARAH ANN BRADLEY.

17 Dec 1844. $20 Reward. Absconded on the 8th inst. a negro man named GODFREY, light griff color, about 5' 5", about 35. MAUNSEL WHITE, Plaquemines Parish.

17 Dec 1844. $25 Reward. Ran away from the Velasco Plantation, belonging to R. A. WILKINSON, in Parish of Plaquemines, 40 miles below the city, on the 10th inst., the slave NED, property of T. O. STARK. He is stout, strong built. He formerly was owned at Old River near Fort Adams. It is supposed he accompanied the slave GODFREY who is owned by Joseph B. Wilkinson.

31 Dec 1844. $5 reward. Ran away, a slave named EMELIA, aged 14, very light color, about 5' 3", slender, straight hair. She speaks French and English.

1 Jan 1845. $5 Reward. Ran away the 20th ult. a slave named EMELIA, aged 14 years, very light color, about 5' 3", slender made, with straight hair and good features. Speaks French and English. I. D. TOWNSEND.

3 Jan 1845. $10 Reward. Ran away on the 28th of December from my place on the Red River, opposite the mouth of the Black River, the griff man DICK GRIFFIN, about 30, thick lips, always laughs or smiles when spoken to, about 5' 9". Was bought of Mark Davis last month and is just imported from Virginia. J. B. MAILET.

15 Jan 1845. $25 Reward. Ran away last May a negro man named FEVRIER, about 35, stout built, very black. JOHN RABASSA.

22 Jan 1845. $10 Reward. Absconded last October from McDonoughville, the woman ESTHER, a griffe, about 5' 4", speaks English fluently and a little French. She is about 24. WILLIAM BUTLER.

4 Feb 1845. $20 Reward. Will be paid for apprehension of a Negro boy named HENRY or HARRY, about 5' 5", 17. Speaks English and French fluently, well built, a scar on his forehead. JOHN B. GRAYSON.

4 Feb 1845. $5 Reward for the black boy SIMON, 4' 3", stoop shouldered and rather humpbacked. JOHN E. HYDE.

14 Feb 1845. $10 Reward. Left the schooner Cornelia at the New Basin, the black boy JACK, about 21, 5' 7". D. W. STARK.

15 Feb 1845. $10 Reward. Ran away about 2 weeks since, a negro woman named JANE, about 35, stout built, stoop shouldered, speaks quick, and has lost some front teeth. A. D. MARVEL.

19 Feb 1845. $10 Reward. Ran away, 2 negro men: WILEY, about 24, 5' 6", heavy built, 175 pounds, small eyes. The other boy JOHN is about 21, about 5' high, stoop shouldered. THOMAS B. YOUNGBLOOD.

25 Feb 1845. $40 Reward. Ran away from her mistress the 17th inst. the negro woman SUSAN, about 22, very black, round face, exhibits the broken English dialect of the African raised in Charleston, S. C. where the race associates much

together and from whence she was brought. GEORGE A. BOTTS.

25 Feb 1845. $10 Reward. Ran away a dark mulatto named COLIN, 25, 5' 4". He speaks French and English. JOHN RABASSA.

26 Feb 1845. $10 Reward. Will be paid for recovery of the black boy NAME, about 22, who absconded about 6 weeks ago. A. BLAKE.

28 Feb 1845. $20 Reward. Ran away from the plantation of Madame Tureaud, in St. James parish my negro boy DAVID, about 25, 6', of a griff color; is a fine looking and genteel servant, very plausible. JESSE HART.

28 Feb 1845. $10 Reward. Ran away the 21st instant, the negro man named JAMES CORSEY, 35, 5 feet 9 inches high. J. B. RODRIQUE, Donaldsonville, La.

4 Mar 1845. $50 Reward. Ran away from Carrollton 22 February the boy JACOB, about 24, 5' 8". Supposed to have run off to Texas or Mobile; also JIM, aged 40, 5' 10", walks stiff from effects of rheumatism in his back. A. B. HINGHAM.

4 Mar 1845. $10 Reward for recovery of my boy NARRY, about 22, who absconded about 6 weeks ago. Narry speaks French and English.

4 Mar 1845. $10 Reward. Ran away on 28th February a negro woman named NANCY, about 40, 5' 6", stout built, and has lost sight of one of her eyes.

5 Mar 1845. $10 Reward. Ran away from Franklin Hall SIMON, a negro man about 19, 5' 6", smooth face, good teeth, round shouldered. He is a cook. L. A. CALDWELL.

7 Mar 1845. $50 Reward. Ran away the 29th of June last, my negro man JOHN, about 5' 7", good front teeth, a bricklayer by trade. I purchased him from James E. Zuntz 2 years ago and he bought him from a Mr. Ensign of Mobile. J. M. ROBERTSON, Mobile.

21 Mar 1845. $10 Reward. For a mulatto boy named CARY, 13 years old, 4 feet 6 inches tall, stout built.

22 Mar 1845. $10 Reward. For the negro woman ELIZA, about 50, 5' 6", high cheek bones and good figure, with her child, 4 years old, a bright mulatto named VICTORIA. J. McGOVERN, Layfayette, La.

23 Mar 1845. $100 reward will be paid for the griff boy ROBERT, about 22, 5' 7". He formerly belonged to Dr. Davezac of this city. PETER TELLON.

26 Mar 1845. $50 Reward. Absconded from the plantation of Mrs. Joseph Melancon, St. James Parish, the yellow man BOUKA, 35, middle size, speaks French and English. J. A. BRAUD.

2 Apr 1845. Was committed to the West Feliciana jail a slave, LOUIS PHILIP, who says he belongs to Henry Copman of New Orleans. JOHN H. HAND, Dep. Sheriff.

3 Apr 1845. $10 Reward. Ran away April 1st the negro woman WINNY, 35 to 40 years old, rather stout built, has a downcast look. JOHN COCHRAN.

5 Apr 1845. $10 Reward. Ran away yesterday a bright mulatto boy apparently 16 years old, straight black hair. His name is JIM. C. F. SNOWDEN.

5 Apr 1845. $40 Reward. Left the steamer Yazoo City where he was hired, on 14 March, the negro man called JOHN DYGS, about 23, 5' 6", copper colored. E. P. SHALL.

5 Apr 1845. $50 Reward. Ran away from the subscriber about 18 March, the mulatto man HUBBARD, aged 26, and lately introduced from Virginia. Mrs. S. STEWART.

5 Apr 1845. $15 Reward. Ran away on the 9th, my negro boy CUDJOE, very black. 5' 7", speaks Indian and very broken English. Has a wild appearance. NAPOLEON B. HAWKINS.

17 Apr 1845. Captains of vessels are cautioned not to employ the negro man ISAAC, alias JOHN BRICE. He is short, thick set, and very black. EDWARD C. CARTER.

25 Apr 1845. $20 Reward. Ran away from the towboat Caledonia the 12th inst. the negro man CHARLES, 28, 5' 6", stout built, slightly bowlegged.

25 Apr 1845. $20 reward will be paid for delivery of the mulatto boy BEN, about 5' 4", very light complexion, narrow chin, high cheek bones.

25 Apr 1845. $20 Reward. Ran away from the plantation of the subscriber in Parish of Plaquemines, on the 14th of January, an American negro named WILLIAM. He is about 25, 5' 4", reddish skin and very bandylegged. ADOLPH REGGIO.

10 May 1845. $25 reward for delivery of JOHN NELSON, who ran away 19 November last. He is about 30, light complexion, and has a slouching gait. JAMES BROWNLEE.

10 May 1845. $20 reward for the yellow girl MARY ANNE, 30, 5' 2", very black hair, well made and strongly built. Has a little of the Indian look. EVARISTE BLANC.

11 May 1845. $10 reward will be paid for delivery of the negro man EDMOND, 27, 5' 11", of a dark copper color, long straight hair. J. A. BEARD.

13 May 1845. $10 Reward. Ran away the 10th inst. the griff boy BOB, about 19, 5' high, stout made, laughs when spoken to, has a scar on his neck. J. GUISHONNET.

13 May 1845. $5 Reward. Ran away from my plantation in Neshoba Co., Miss., on Christmas night, a negro named TOM, about 30 years old, square made, small sunken eyes. He reads well and perhaps writes some. W. W. BELL.

15 May 1845. $10 Reward. Ran away the 10th inst. the yellow girl ANN, about 20, middle size, dresses rather neat, and usually wears a headkerchief. JOHN A. STEVENSON.

21 May 1845. $10 Reward. Ran away the 3d inst. the negro boy JACK, 18, about 5' 4", very black, good countenance. He is a house servant and has never done anything else. P. M. TOURNE.

22 May 1845. $10 Reward. Ran away from the Louisiana state boat Experiment, the boy WILLIAM BRADLEY, 29, light black, stout made; joint of forefinger on left hand is off. The above reward will be paid by the State Engineer's office.

23 May 1845. $10 Reward. will be given for delivery of the slave SARAH LOCKWOOD, a Creole, about 20, to the undersigned or to D. Augustin, Sheriff of the Parish Court. She is of ordinary height and is believed to be pregnant.

29 May 1845. $50 Reward. Ran away about 7 weeks ago, a negro boy named HENRY, 11 or 12 years old. He formerly belonged to Dr. Halsey, of Vicksburg. The above reward will be paid to whoever will deliver the boy to Alex Verdelet of Vicksburg.

29 May 1845. $10 Reward for the negro woman QUEEN, who ran away the 20th inst. She is middle sized, between 40 and 45, black complexion, high cheek bones, flat nose, and has lost her upper front teeth. SAMUEL BELL.

29 May 1845. $10 Reward. Ran away on the 21st the negro boy HENRY, a dark griff, large eyes, about 20, 5' 5". JOHN McCLEAN.

6 Jun 1845. $10 Reward for a negro woman called HANNAH, who ran away last month. She is about 50, is 5' 6", and very slender. She has lost her right eye.

6 Jun 1845. Ran away from the plantation of Col. Maunsel White, Plaquemines parish, the negro boy GEORGE GUY. He is about 5' 6", of a dark griff color, lame in one leg and had on when he left an iron collar around his neck, and around one of his legs. MAUNSEL WHITE.

10 Jun 1845. $20 Reward. Ran away the 31st of May, the boy named WILLIAM, of middle size, stout, has a scar in the shape of a crescent on his forehead. He formerly belonged to Mrs. Widow Halphen. E. SIMON.

11 Jun 1845. $40 reward will be paid for delivery of the following negroes who ran away from my plantation near Fort Pike, La., on the 3d inst. PHIL--40 years old, dark complexion. SAM--20 years old, has a scar on his chin. ALEXANDER GEORGE.

15 Jun 1845. $100 Reward. For delivery of my boy PHILANDER. He is a bright mulatto, 40 years old, 5' 11", has straight black hair, thin face, round shouldered, and by trade a house carpenter. He ran away last October from East Feliciana parish. J. A. VANCE.

17 Jun 1845. $50 reward will be paid for a negro man named CLINTON who absconded on 20 May last. He is about 30, 6 feet high, of reddish complexion. He speaks English and a little French. He ran away once before from Vicksburg, Miss. LUCIEN LABRANCHE.

17 Jun 1845. $25 Reward. Ran away 7th June the black boy named LUCIEN, belonging to Mr. O. H. Miesegaes of this city. He is strong and well built, about 5' 6", has an acquiline nose, and speaks French and English. CHARLES KOCK.

17 Jun 1845. $5 Reward. Absconded on Sunday night the negro boy PETER, 18, about 5' 4", stout built. He has a scar on one ear. JOHN G. GREEVES.

20 Jun 1845. $20 Reward. Ran away the 17th inst. a negro woman named HARRIET, 24, 5' 6". Has a defect on one cheek. GEORGE JAQUES.

22 Jun 1845. $50 Reward. Ran away Wednesday last the negro boy DAVE or DAVID, 26 years old. Took with him a gold lever watch and 3 pairs of new boots. JESSE HART.

2 Jul 1845. $10 Reward. Ran away the negro boy, BOSTON, 12, reddish hair, very flat nose. He speaks English only. He was bought from Mr. J. Hagan. VICTOR MARTIN.

10 Jul 1845. $100 Reward. Ran away from my plantation in the parish of St. John the Baptist, the slave MATHY, a griff about 38, and his wife, LITTY, black, about 35. They were formerly owned in Alabama and may head there. M. B. HAYDEL.

13 Jul 1845. $5 Reward. Ran away the 8th inst. the griffe negress MARY, alias ELLEN, about 25, 5' 3" tall. Speaks English only.

20 July 1845. $20 Reward. Ran away on the 17th inst. a negro boy named HAMLET or HAMILTON, about 24 years old, 5' 7" tall. He was purchased in Alabama. L. B. WRIGHT.

22 Jul 1845. $5 Reward. To whoever will arrest the negro man DANIEL, who ran away from 172 Royal st. He is about 5' 6" high and belongs to F. M. Bienvenu. Daniel always changes his name and has a false pass, as he can read and write. He has 2 scars on his cheek, which he made himself to hide the word, "runaway".

23 Jul 1845. $50 Reward. Ran away 1st July, the mulatto boy JACK, 28, 5' 5" high, curly hair, freckled face, speaks French and English. He formerly belonged to Seaman Field. ORRAN BYRD.

25 Jul 1845. $10 Reward. Ran away from the plantation of Jules Villiere the 23d inst. a mulatto woman named RACHEL, aged 22 years, has a full round face and a little beard on the upper lip. She speaks French and English. CHARLES RITCHIE.

26 Jul 1845. $25 reward for apprehension of the griff man JIM, about 5' 3" tall, has a scar on his right jaw. Speaks English only. J. R. NOBLE.

27 Jul 1845. $10 Reward. Ran away on 23 July a negro girl named SARAH, sometimes called SALLY, about 5' 2" tall, and very stout. Talks fast and smiles when she speaks. JOHN S. AITKENS.

30 Jul 1845. $20 Reward. Ran away on 1st of June, from William H. Morgan, in Plaquemines parish, the slave NANCY, a bright mulatto about 25, 5' 3" high; has black curly hair, nearly straight. She came to New Orleans from Mississippi.

31 Jul 1845. $25 Reward for the negro boy WILLIAM or BILL, aged 23 years. He is about 5' 10" and weighs about 180 pounds. Has a stab mark on his right side and his back shows marks of a severe whipping. He sometimes answers to the name of JOB. BENNETT & EAGER.

1 Aug 1845. $20 Reward. Ran away from in July the negro girl ANNA or MORGIANA, about 4' 2", flat nose, high cheek bones. M. BOULIGNY.

1 Aug 1845. $25 Reward. Ran away from the premises of AUGUSTE LAGORY in Vicksburg, on 18 July, the negro boy ISAAC, about 18, 5' 6" high, of a dark yellowish complexion. He was lately purchased of T. G. DAVIDSON, in Livingston, La., who purchased him from BOYD WILLIAMS of Clinton, La.

3 Aug 1845. $20 Reward for apprehension of the negro man SOLOMON, who ran away from my plantation near

Holmesville, Pike Co., Miss., on 20th April last. He is about 40, black, somewhat bald, of low stature, stutters badly, and is marked with the lash. JOHN T. LAMKIN.

6 Aug 1845. $20 reward for delivery of the negro man WILLIAM, alias KINCAID, who ran away the 3d inst. He is about 35, 5' 6" tall, of a brownish color. FRERET BROTHERS.

16 Aug 1845. $10 Reward. Ran away the 10th, the slave ROBERT, about 16, very black, tall and slender. He is a Creole and speaks French and English. He lisps a little. WILLIAM LEECH.

17 Aug 1845. $5 Reward. I caution the public against harboring my slave ROBERT MONTEGUT, a slater by trade. PETER DALY.

20 Aug 1845. Ran away from W. J. Minor's plantation, the 17th inst. the black boy FRENCH, about 16, small and slender. His mother lives in this city. He is well known as a race rider.

21 Aug 1845. $5 Reward. Absconded the 18th, the negro boy WALLACE or WILLIAM WALLACE, about 19 years, 5' 10", large bony form. Has been employed in cotton presses. W. E. TURNER.

26 Aug 1845. $200 Reward. Stolen from my plantation near Utica, Hinds Co, Miss., on the 27th ultimo, the following negroes. JIM, 24 years old, 5' 9", dark complexion, right hand cut off at the wrist, was brought from Kentucky last fall. ROSANA, wife to JIM, aged 17, copper color. CHARLES, aged 18, dark color, cross-eyed, 5' 7" tall. HENDERSON, black, 26 years old, 5' 6" tall. R. NUTT.

27 Aug 1845. $25 Reward. Ran away from the plantation of ANTOINE BOUDOUSQUIE, St. John the Baptist parish, a mulatto man named GEORGE WHITE, of ordinary height; has small bright eyes, small mouth, intelligent face.

28 Aug 1845. $20 Reward for delivery in any jail of the boy TOM, a negro, 28, 5' 10" tall. I purchased him 3 months since from Mr. Hugh Lewis, of Madison Co., Miss. GEORGE A. BOTTS.

4 Sep 1845. $20 Reward for apprehension of my negro man ABRAHAM, very black, about 30, 5' 9" tall. Has lost some front teeth; quick and intelligent. I purchased him from John Lamkin, of Mississippi 2 months since. SAMUEL L. MOSES.

7 Sep 1845. $20 Reward. Supposed to have been enticed away by some white men on 2d inst. a negro girl named SARAH, 12 or 13 years old, a scar on her left hand. O. A. BLISS.

20 Sep 1845. $15 Reward. Ran away on the 18th a mulatto boy named CHARLES, about 13, 4' 5" tall.

1 Oct 1845. $10 reward will be paid for lodging in any jail the negro man TONEY or TONY. He is about 24, tall and spare made, walks lame. Ran away on the 1st inst. from a plantation in St. Charles Parish.

12 Oct 1845. $20 Reward. Left the subscriber's dwelling on 22 Sep. the black slave woman AMEE, aged 32, 5' 8", broad, square shoulders, walks lame. She was a dry goods marchand in the city for several years. WILLIAM H. MARTIN.

16 Oct 1845. $10 Reward. Ran away 14 Sep. the griffe girl ELIZA, aged 25, has a blue mark on her temple, is about 5' 6" high. WILLIAM T. THOMPSON.

16 Oct. 1845. $5 Reward. Ran away on the 12th inst. the griffe girl VENUS, aged about 30. AUGUST BLOOM.

19 Oct 1845. $10 Reward. Absconded 3 weeks since, the negro slave HIRAM, 5' 2", stout built, thick lips, speaks French and English. He is about 30 years old. JULES A. BLANC.

24 Oct 1845. $50 Reward. Left my plantation 20 October, in Fort Pike, La., two slaves. PHIL, about 35, black; was purchased from Samuel Vaughn of Florence, Ala. JIM, 28, 5' 9", was purchased from Major Atkinson of Augusta, Ga. ALEXANDER GEORGE.

5 Nov 1845. $20 Reward. Ran away from my plantation in St. Charles parish a mulatto man, CAMDEN, about middle size, genteel appearance, good figure, respectful manners. Had on good clothes and a blue overcoat of the U. S. A. uniform. CHARLES OXLEY.

5 Nov 1845. $5 reward for apprehension of the slave JOHN LAMAR, 5' 6", 30, ears pierced for rings, speaks English and French. He left my domicile, parish of Iberville, Bayou Gros Tete, on August 24th. Jim was purchased of Mr. Pincard. AUSTIN WOOLFOLK.

7 Nov 1845. $200 Reward. Ran away from the plantation of Mrs. Aune E. Shepherd, Stewart Co., Ga., about Nov. 1st, her negro man GILBERT, a tall black, no front teeth, a first rate cook and waiter, about 33. Also from the same place her boy AUSTIN, 18, of light complexion.

12 Nov 1845. $20 Reward. For apprehension of the negress CHARLOTTE, a light griffe, short and thick set, small eyes. She is far gone in pregnancy. Charlotte was a fruit seller. She speaks French and English. E. C. CARTER.

26 Nov 1845. $10 Reward. Ran away on 5th inst. the negro man PETE; has lost his left arm; is a painter by trade, 5' 9", about 30. DAVID MORES.

28 Nov 1845. $10 Reward. Ran away on the 22nd inst. the negro boy JIM about 30, 5' 9", dark griff complexion. He works as a tobacco cooper. RICHARD CHARLES.

28 Nov 1845. $10 Reward. Ran away the 8th inst. the yellow man SANDY, 25, 5' 7". He is a house servant and cook, and also a whitewasher and brick layer, and very intelligent. H. F. WADE.

7 Dec 1845. $5 reward will be paid for apprehension of the slave LOUISA, a light negress, aged about 28, ordinary height, speaks French and English. WILLIAM T. THOMPSON.

9 Dec 1845. $10 Reward. Ran away from the boarding house of Mrs. Barney, the boy JACK, about 16, small and quick in his movements. L. A. CALDWELL.

16 Dec 1845. $75 Reward. Absconded the 11th inst. the negro boy MORRIS, about 25, nearly 6' high, weighs 160 to 170 pounds. He is well known as a drayman, and speaks French and English. E. P. SHALL.

16 Dec 1845. $5 Reward will be paid for delivery of the mulatto girl ABBY, 5' 8", small scar over her left eye, slightly freckled, has a fine set of teeth. G. B. ANTHONY.

19 Dec 1845. $25 reward will be paid for apprehension of my slave JOHN EDWARDS, a dark mulatto, about 5' 11" tall. He says his wife belongs to a cashier at one of the city's banks. He is a good body servant. AUGUSTIN PUGH, Donaldsonville, La.

19 Dec 1845. $20 Reward. Ran away, EDWARD, a mulatto boy, 14, has black straight hair of a natural curl. He was formerly owned by S. Turner of this city. GEORGE A. BOTTS.

20 Dec 1845. $25 Reward will be given for my mulatto boy WILLIAM who ran away on the 15th inst. He is about 25, and can read and write. J. LE CESNE.

20 Dec 1845. $50 Reward. Ran away in Sep. or Oct. a black slave named MOSE or MOSES (belonging to Mrs. D. Dayton, Rifle Point, La.) 28, 5' 9", slow of speech, reddish eyes. EDWARD COCHRAN.

27 Dec 1845. $10 reward will be paid for information leading to recovery of the slave FANNY and her daughter MATILDA, last seen on the 25th inst. Fanny is about 25, speaks French and English; Matilda is about 4 years old, speaks French and a little English. Apply to the office of the Picayune.

4 Jan 1846. $100 Reward. Ran away on 26 Dec. a mulatto boy named HENRY PHILLIPS, about 17, 5' 5", handsome features, long hair. He is a first rate body servant. He weighs about 130 lbs. He has been owned by Dr. McFarlane, Dr. Porter and Sewal T. Turner, all of this city. Ran away from the plantation of Hippolyte Tregpagnier about 6 months ago. Also

the creole mulatto boy named CELESTIN, about 32, 5' 7", front teeth out. CAMPBELL & LABRANCHE.

10 Jan 1846. $15 Reward. Ran away the 20th ultimo from Eureka Plantation, Iberville Parish, the mulatto HENRY WILSON, 35 to 40, small stature, has no back teeth. He is a good bricklayer, plasterer, and mattress maker. He can read and write well and has some pretensions of preaching. ELLMAKER & SHROPSHIRE.

1 Jan 1846. $10 reward for apprehension of the boy EMERSON, who absconded on the 14th, ultimo. He is about 5' 9", has a goatee under his chin, and is a good looking, slender griff. E. L. TRACY.

3 Feb 1846. $25 Reward. Ran away last month from Parish of St. James a slave man named DICK, about 36, tall and likely. He is left handed, of a dark griff color, has on his breast the letters "J. C.". J. A. BRAUD.

3 Feb 1846. $25 Reward. Left the subscriber the 30th ultimo, the negro girl FELICIANNA or NANCY, about 25 years old and 5' 4" high. GEORGE W. SMITH.

4 Feb 1846. $50 reward for apprehension of the slaves DANIEL and JOE. Daniel is a light colored negro, about 25, 5' 9" tall. Joe, a griff, is about 25 years old, about 5' 10" tall. They can be distinguished by the drawl peculiar to the negroes of South Carolina. S. R. PROCTOR.

6 Feb 1846. $25 Reward. Ran away the boy HENRY CRAWFORD, of a quadroon color, 23, 5' 6", stout and well made; a blacksmith by trade. WILLIAM HARRISON.

6 Feb 1846. $20 Reward. Absconded the 25th of January, the negro boy SAM, about 19, 5' 2" tall. Speaks English and French. ALEX HARRIS.

6 Feb 1846. Ran away the 3d inst. a negro man named BOB, 22, heavy set. He recently was the property of Capt. M. G. Anders. A liberal reward will be paid for his apprehension. LILLARD & MOSBY.

6 Feb 1846. $10 reward will be paid for the mulatto boy WILLIAM, formerly belonging to Mr. Regnier, aged 32. He is 5' 6", thin face, with a black beard, straight hair, speaks French and English. He is a good painter and was a milk seller in the city. C. JUMONVILLE.

10 Feb 1846. $20 Reward. Absconded the 28th of November last, a handsome mulatto girl named KIT, about 16, low stature, full face, bushy hair.

13 Feb 1846. $25 Reward. Ran away, 24 miles from Donaldsonville, La., on Bayou Lafourche, on 29 January, a negro boy named JOHN KEER, 19, 5' 10", dark copper color, 150 to 160 pounds. CARNES & TATE.

14 Feb 1846. $50 Reward. Ran away from the plantation of Col. Stewart of West Baton Rouge about the 1st of Dec. last, a likely black boy named TOM, about 17, 5' 8" tall. He was brought from Virginia by Mr. Peterson last fall.

3 Mar 1846. $10 Reward for apprehension of the negro boy JOE, who ran away yesterday. He is 20 years old, very black, short stature. SAMUEL BELL.

4 Mar 1846. $20 for the delivery of JANE, a negress, 40, stout and black. She was formerly owned by Judge Bogeaurd. She is

a Creole and speaks French and English. GEORGE A. BOTTS.

6 Mar 1846. $20 Reward. Absconded the 20th ultimo, a dark mulatto girl named LOUISA or HETTY, 5' 3" tall, good looking, a scar on her face, a peculiarly fine head of curling hair.

7 Mar 1846. $20 Reward. Ran away a month since, MARIA WHITE, a griffe slave about 18, slender and common size.

14 Mar 1846. $50 reward for apprehension of my boy KING, who ran away on 27 February, living in Mobile, 25, 5' 10" tall, dark complexion. He is a bricklayer by trade and is intelligent. A. BOULWARE.

15 Mar 1846. On 21st February 3 slaves ran away from me in parish of Assumption: WILLIAM, a mulatto, about 35, 6' high, well made. Speaks some French; he is a field hand and ditcher, very industrious. I have owned him for about 10 years. GEORGE SMITH, a mulatto, 19, 6' high, stout built, good looking. George has been my yard servant and carriage driver; he never did anything else since I owned him. I purchased him from Thomas Baudard in June 1845, who brought him from Port Royal, Va. MILES, negro, 5' 10", about 30. He is a whip sawyer and field hand. I purchased him from James A. McHutton in New Orleans in March 1845. He was brought from Missouri. A. M. FOLEY.

18 Mar 1846. $20 Reward. Ran away from the plantation of W. B. KENNER, above the city, a negro man named ISAAC BROWN, 20, quite black and stout, about 5' 10". JAMES T. BLAKENY.

27 Mar 1846. $15 Reward. Ran away yesterday, a mustee about 27 years old named EBENEZER SMITH. Has lost the third finger of his left hand.

27 Mar 1846. $10 Reward. Will be paid for apprehension of the mulatto boy named WILLIAM, formerly belonging, 1st to Mrs. Kennedy, 2d to Mr. O'Callaghan, and 3d to Mr. Regnier. He is 32, 5' 3", long, straight black hair, and speaks French and English. C. JUMONVILLE.

29 Mar 1846. $10 Reward. Ran away 22 Feb. my servant woman CORA, about 26 years old, 5' 6" tall, front teeth gone. JAMES JENKINS.

1 Apr 1846. Ran away 28th ult. the slave OSCAR. He was taken from the chain gang of the 1st Municipality and put to work in Wood's cotton press. He is a yellow, well known creole of this city. SAMUEL DE PASS.

3 Apr 1846. $10 Reward. Ran away on the 21st ult. my servant woman MARY ANN, about 18, of middle size. She speaks French and English. F. Y. PARRA.

3 Apr 1846. $10 Reward. Will be paid for apprehension of a negro man named JERRY, about 40, 5' 2". Speaks good English. He formerly belonged to Christian Katzenberger of Bay St. Louis. He has worked for me as a baker for 4 months. J. A. PRIEUR.

4 Apr 1846. $50 Reward for apprehension of my slave boy JACOB, a light mulatto, 14 years old, slightly knock-kneed. He ran away a month ago. ISAAC PIPKIN.

10 Apr 1846. $50 Reward -- Stop Thief! Was stolen from my plantation 10 miles south of Clinton, La., on the 2d inst. a

bright mulatto aged 25, 6', named ISAAC GARDNER. He reads well, and had a number of books with him. He is a Methodist preacher, and is a blacksmith by trade. R. M. AUSTEN.

10 Apr 1846. $20 Reward. Ran away from me 17 Nov. last a negro woman named LOUISE, 26, few or no teeth, is marked with the whip. She is addicted to drinking. She was acquired of John Leeds of this city and formerly belonged to Madame Edouard Guerin, who now owns Louise's mother. WILLIAM T. THOMPSON.

10 Apr 1846. $25 Reward. Will be paid for detention of MARY ANN, who absconded the last of February. She was purchased from Mr. Mulliken. GUSTAVOS COLHOUN.

12 Apr 1846. $10 Reward. Ran away from her mistress yesterday a negro girl about 17 named MARGARET COLLINS, being acquired of Thomas Boudar last month.

14 Apr 1846. $250 Reward. First: $100 for the runaway negro DAVID or DAVIS, left 4 months ago, about 34, common size, has a great amount of hair on his body. Belonged in 1843 and '44 to Adolph Reggio of Plaquemines parish. He has a wife in this city. Second: $150 for the mulatto man JACQUES or WILSON or VINCENT, 40, absent several years, 5' 8", has a dog bite scar on one leg. P. J. WEEKS, St. James Parish.

15 Apr 1846. $10 Reward. Ran away from Mobile, Ala., the 1st inst. the mulatto slave WILLIAM, belonging to Mrs. A. Sands, 5' 8", stout built.

16 Apr 1846. Stolen on the 18th of March, 1 mile below Natchez, a black boy named BILL, 14, slight built. O. K. FIELD, Natchez.

16 Apr 1846. $50 Reward for the negro girl MARTHA or MATILDA, absent since 10th inst. She is blind in the right eye, is about 28, and slim. She was formerly owned by M. L. Pesigo in 1844; by James Carter of Algiers, in '43; by C. J. Allen in '42, and by P. Hanson in '41. Also the slave STEPHEN, 35, 5' 7", slim figure. He was owned in 1843 by A. H. Donalson; by G. R. Beard in '42; by G. W. Patterson in '42; by John Rodes in '41 and Edward Lombard in '40. SAMUEL STEWART.

26 Apr 1846. $10 Reward. Ran away the 15th, the negro woman JULIA, 30, middle size, light griffe color. She formerly belonged to Mr. Hoffman, coachmaker, of Rampart st. HENRY FERRIS.

28 Apr 1846. $10 Reward. Ran away 23 April, a negro woman JUDY, 40, 5' 6", griffe color, gray hair, long chin. L. LAMBERT.

2 May 1846. $10 Reward. Ran away last month my slave HENRY, about 5' 7", dark complexion, stout made. JULES DRUILKET.

3 May 1846. $15 Reward will be paid for the mulatto slave, FREDERIC, who absconded 3 weeks ago. He belongs to Mr. Alphonse Prehon, and speaks French and English.

15 May 1846. $100 Reward. Ran away from the steamer F. M. Streck on 2 April, 2 negro men: JOHN KNIGHT, very likely, about 5' 8", aged 24, speaks quick and uses good language. HENRY, about 5' 10", slightly marked by smallpox. W. C. WILSON.

17 May 1846. $10 Reward will be paid for the mulatto boy HENRY or MONTGOMERY, who absconded the 7th inst. He is of light build, 5' 7", aged about 18, and is slightly cross-eyed. JOSEPH H. MOORE.

20 May 1846. $10 Reward for the negro man MORRIS who ran away on the 11th inst. He is about 25, is 6' tall, and weighs about 160 pounds. He is known as a drayman in the city. E. P. SHALL.

22 May 1846. $50 Reward. Ran away in February, 3 slaves, 16 miles below Thibodauxville, La. NELSON TURNER, 6' high, aged 50. We bought him last June from Branch W. Lee, Cumberland Court House, Va. DAVE GLOVER, copper colored, 25, 5' 10". We bought him from Mr. Grady in Richmond, Va., last July. TOM WONSLY, aged 25, 5' 8". We bought him last July from Mr. Cochran of Richmond, Va. PUGH & TUCKER, La Fourche Interior.

27 May 1846. $60 Reward. Ran away 2 months since from my plantation at Barrataria, Jefferson parish, 3 slaves: CLEM, a negro about 5' 7", aged 25. NED, a griffe, 5' 11", aged 45, has a mark on his breast. JOHN, an old negro, long hair, 5' 7", formerly belonged to William Jones of Carrollton. J. DAVIS Jr.

27 May 1846. $20 Reward. Ran away from my plantation 20 miles above New Orleans on the 20th inst. 3 negroes, recently form Virginia: HARRISON, tall and slender, 20, upper joint of right thumb missing. SAM CAMPBELL, 6' broad shoulders, aged 25. JANET, a griff boy, 20, about 5' 4" tall. WILLIAM POLK.

28 May 1846. $25 Reward. Ran away from my plantation, parish of St. James, the 24th inst. 2 slaves--DAVID TAYLOR, aged 25, about 5' 9", dark complexion. LEWIS, a griff, about

24, 5' 9". I bought David Taylor in March 1845 from N. F. Slatter, and Lewis from Mr. D. Gandet in January. Mr. Gandet purchased Lewis from Mack Davis. VALRY GANDET.

28 May 1846. $30 Reward. Will be paid for apprehension of the mulatto boy ELLICK, or ALEXANDER, 5' 9". Speaks French, English, and Spanish. He left the steamboat Oreline last February. He formerly belonged to the estate of E. C. FERGUSON, dec'd. P. H. GLAZE.

16 June 1846. $25 Reward. Ran away, the negro BROWN, well known as a bread seller in the 2d Municipality, about 5' 6", strong built, heavy whiskers. D'AQUIN BROTHERS.

18 Jun 1846. $10 Reward. Ran away yesterday the negro girl LIDDY or LYDIA, 19, a likely servant, speaks English and broken French. I bought her last month from the estate of Mrs. Barbay. HENRY ST. PAUL.

21 Jun 1846. $10 Reward. Ran away from the steamer Paul Jones last week a negro boy named ALBERT or ALFRED, 23, 6'. I purchased him from Mr. R. Fettington. He was raised in Nashville, Tenn. W. A. BENNETT.

24 Jun 1846. $25 Reward. Ran away from Mr. Lucien Labranche's plantation in Jefferson parish, a negro slave named JOHN DUSNAN, 40, 5' 9". CLEMENT BROWN.

27 Jun 1846. $100 Reward for RACHAL, a mulatto girl, 14, 4' 9", long bushy hair. She has been here 7 months and is very intelligent. E. LOCKETT.

1 Jul 1846. $25 Reward. Will be paid by the State Engineer's office for arresting the boy POMPEY WILLIAMS, who left the State boat Franklin on June 21. He is about 5' 4", aged 26,

light black color, thick set. WILLIAM MAYO, State Engineer.

1 Jul 1846. $200 Reward for the mulatto man named JOHN, employed last winter as waiter at Hewlett's Hotel and then as a cook by Mr. Bayliss. John is almost white. He has wooly hair, is about 5' 7" tall. He was pruchased last year from Mr. Peterson, and formerly belonged to Mr. Parker, in Natchez. He has been in New Orleans for 5 or 6 years. He has a wife in Cincinnati. Dr. Monroe Mackie.

1 Jul 1846. $20 Reward. Ran away from the plantation of Judge La Branch, St. Charles Parish, on 29 June, the griff boy JOE, belonging to Mr. O. O. St. Aman.

7 Jul 1846. $20 Reward. Absconded, the slave BETSY, about 4' 9", speaks French and English, has lost the last 2 fingers of her right hand. JOHN NEWBERRY.

7 Jul 1846. $250 Reward. Ran away or was stolen on 8 June, a black man called EMANUEL, a blacksmith by trade, slender made, has polished manners. JOHN S. GLIDDEN.

14 Jul 1846. Absconded. The negro boy PETER, 16, has been some 12 months a cook on the schooner Emma in Mobile. He is short and fat, has decayed teeth. $50 reward will be paid for his delivery in the calaboose. B. W. HUNTINGTON.

14 Jul 1846. $20 Reward. Ran away on 28 June, PETER, a negro man 6', 25 years old, slender made. Peter was raised in South Carolina, and has been but a short time in the city. JOHN HARRALL.

14 Jul 1846. $200 Reward. Ran away last November a white negro man almost 35, 5' 8", blue eyes, yellow woolly head,

very fair skin. Has an ugly scar on his breast from the kick of a horse. He was raised in Columbia, S. C., and is known by the name DICK FRAZIER. He lately worked on the railroad in Alabama and passed as a white man named Jesse Teams. He is a good butcher, horse-breeder, house-painter, cook, white-washer, and hoe maker. J. D. ALLEN, Barnwell Court House, S. C.

14 Jul 1846. The following negroes ran away on the 12th inst. BILL, or LOUIS, about 5' 4", very black, bright skin. He speaks English well, French slightly. CHARLES, a griff, 5' 4", speaks English. FRANK, a negro, has large eyes. He speaks only English. PITT, or PETER, well made, yellowish hue, front teeth decayed. He speaks French and English. A reward of $10 will be paid for each of them. D. POINCY & CO.

16 Jul 1846. $20 Reward will be paid for apprehension of a negro girl named MARGARET, 12, 4' 4", black complexion, woolly hair, very intelligent; speaks French and English.

17 Jul 1846. $10 Reward. Ran away the 6th instant the black boy JOHN BULL, 30, 5' 4", badly marked by smallpox. Has a scar produced by his attempt to cut his throat. I bought him from a Mr. Miller, 9 months ago. GEORGE G. KIRK.

21 Jul 1846. $15 Reward. Ran away the 10th inst. the yellow boy named JOE, 2 front teeth gone, well known in the city as a drummer. P. A. DUBORD.

21 Jul 1846. Was committed to jail on 21 April last a negro man named TOM, who says he belongs to Charles Coffey, 2 miles from New Orleans. He is about 40, 5' 11", light hair, is a good cook and can read some. Says he was born free but sold

in New Orleans when about 7 years old, and formerly followed the sea. C. CRINE, Canton, Miss.

22 Jul 1846. $30 Reward will be paid to whoever returns to me the following slaves--LIZA, an American mulatto, 5' 5", 30 years old. LOUISA, daughter of LIZA, 14, 5' tall, speaks French and English, darker than her mother. Both formerly belonged to Mr. Solomon High. ARTHUR FORTIER.

22 Jul 1846. $10 Reward. Ran away yesterday a negro man, PETER, a painter by trade, left arm off just above the elbow joint, 6' tall. D. MORRES, Lafayette, La.

25 Jul 1846. $10 Reward. Ran away last June, the slave NELSON, 5' 8 or 9" tall, 28 years old. Has lost part of his right hand forefinger. He was purchased from Gorin & Smith of New Orleans and came from Red River County, Texas. J. A. BEARD.

25 Jul 1846. Ran away from me, living 27 miles west of Shreveport, La., in Caddo parish, 25 Nov. last, a negro named GEORGE, 27, 5' 11", between a copper and black color. He is a shoemaker. He was raised in Amite County, Miss. THOMAS L. TALBERT.

28 Jul 1846. $10 Reward. Ran away 21 July a negro man called WILLIAM WASHINGTON, about 5' 6" high, 26 years old. Has a knife scar on one arm. E. J. GARDNER.

30 Jul 1846. $10 Reward. Ran away a week since, the griff boy HENRY TAYLOR, 25, middle size, irregular teeth. DANA RODGERS.

31 Jul 1846. $10 Reward will be paid for information to recover the negro man GRUNDY, tall, slim and black, aged 20. GREEN & McDOUGALL.

11 Aug 1846. $10 Reward. absconded on 2d inst. the slave HANA or ANN LEE, black, 5' 2", very stout, speaks only English. CATHERINE McMULLEN.

11 Aug 1846. $50 Reward. Absconded on the 7th, the mulatto boy GEORGE, 24, 5' 7". Has one leg reduced since boyhood. CHARLES MOORE.

15 Aug 1846. $20 Reward. Ran away from the steamboat DeSoto, a deck hand named GEORGE, or BAPTISTE, 5' 6", aged 20, speaks French and English. He is a mulatto. ALEX PHILIPS.

20 Aug 1846. $5 Reward. Ran away 17th inst. the black boy JIM, alias JAMES PENN, 25, 5' 4", chunky build, limps a little. T. O. TILGHMAN.

21 Aug 1846. $20 Reward. Ran away from my plantation 26 miles above New Orleans on the 11th inst. a negro boy named JOE, recently from Virginia, 20, 5' 5", very stout; and BOB, 20, 5' 9", very likely. W. POLK.

21 Aug 1846. $50 Reward will be paid for apprehension of a yellow man named JOE McMULLEN. He was formerly drummer for the Volunteers. He speaks, reads and writes English. He has curly hair and is about 5' 6" tall. P. A. DUBORD.

23 Aug 1846. $40 Reward will be paid for arrest of the following negroes who absconded from the plantation of Jean Derou, Ascension parish, on the 17th instant: WILEY, 21, 6',

speaks English only. GEORGE, 28, speaks English only. They were bought in New Orleans from George Davis on 22 June. J. A. BRAUD.

25 Aug 1846. $25 Reward. Ran away yesterday the bright mulatto boy MIKE, 23, 5' 10", a cooper in the tobacco warehouse. C. D. YANCEY.

25 Aug 1846. $40 Reward. Ran away the 23d inst. the yellow woman SARAH, 25, tall and slim.

26 Aug 1846. $15 Reward. Ran away from my plantation in Iberville parish on 22d inst. 2 negroes--SAM, a dark griff, 5' 5", thick set; GEORGE, a bright mulatto, 26, 5' 5". L. MONTGOMERY.

30 Aug 1846. $10 Reward. The mulatto boy EDWARD ran away from the plantation of Joseph E. Whitall, near Plaquemine, on the 2d inst. He is about 20, 4' 11" tall, speaks English and French. ADAMS & McCALL.

4 Sep 1846. $25 Reward. Ran away from the plantation of Madame Fergus Duplantier, near Manchac, in June, a bright mulatto named NED, 5' 11", about 35, speaks French and English. May try to pass as a white man as he has sandy hair of a clear color.

11 Sep 1846. $50 Reward. Absconded July, 1845, the griffe girl named MARY ELLEN, 5' 3" tall, about 26, stout built.

11 Sep 1846. $15 Reward. Ran away the slave HENRY, 21, very plausible, sometimes calls himself ROBERT. JOHN DORE.

11 Sep 1846. $10 Reward. Ran away in August the slave ALBERT, a dark griff, aged 35, about 5' 5". GEORGE REED.

12 Sep 1846. $20 Reward. Ran away 27 June from my plantation at Barrataria, Jefferson parish, the griff slave, NED, 45, 4' 11". Has a mark on his left breast. J. DAVIS JR.

16 Sep 1846. $50 Reward. Ran away 24 August from me on Bayou Goula, Iberville parish, a negro man GEORGE, 28, 5' 9", black complexion, a carpenter by trade. JOHN H. RANDOLPH.

23 Sep 1846. $20 Reward for the mulatto POLLY, alias MARY CRISWELL, about 55. She ran away the 7th instant. ELIZABETH PRICE.

23 Sep 1846. $25 Reward. Ran away the slave WILLIAM or JOHN (as he calls himself). He is 21, about 170 pounds, broad shouldered, well formed. He was brought from Charleston, S. C., 2 months ago. He is remarkable for his good looks. WILLIAM BLEAKLEY.

26 Sep 1846. $100 Reward. Ran away from Lafayette, La., in Jefferson parish, on the 23d inst. a dark griff named PLEASANT, about 6' tall, 27 years old. He ran away 5 years ago and went to Cincinnati. Z. DOWTY.

1 Oct 1846. $10 Reward. Ran away the mulatto HENRI alias BENJAMIN, 5' 1", speaks French and English, and writes English. Light complexion. Formerly belonged to Mr. Come Marthesseau.

2 Oct 1846. $60 Reward. Ran away from my plantation 4 miles from Thibodaux, La., on the 13th ultimate, 4 negro men--JOHN RANDOLPH, a griff, 5' 10", slender build.

HENRY ARMSTRONG, a griff, 30, 6' and stout. FOUNTAIN or THORNTON, a black, 6' 2", 30, third finger of left hand cut off. ISOM or ISAAC, black, 5' 6', 28. They were brought from Kentucky last year. BENJAMIN CROSS.

3 Oct 1846. $40 Reward will be paid for apprehension of the negro boy WILLIAM WALLACE, 19, 5' 10", large frame. W. E. TURNER.

8 Oct 1846. $5 Reward. Ran away from my plantation in St. James parish, 25 Sep., a griff boy AMOS, 35, 5' 3", speaks French and English. He formerly belonged to John S. David of Jefferson parish. SOSTHEFFLE ROMAN.

10 Oct 1846. $10 Reward. Will be given for apprehension of the griffe woman EDEY, who absconded the 6th inst. She speaks French and English; of small stature, has a slight scar on her face and hands. She use to sell bouquets. B. CORNU.

11 Oct 1846. $5 Reward. Absconded on Thursday, the black boy MARCH, about 5' 6", stutters badly. Mr. McFREELY.

18 Oct 1846. $150 reward. Was stolen from me on 25 August, a light black woman called MARY JANE. Has very bad front teeth. She is about 5' 2", 27 years old, and a little deaf. JAMES M. BRABSTON, Vicksburg.

18 Oct 1846. $50 Reward. Ran away about 16 Sep., the black girl SARAH, 24, 5' 3", slender frame, large eyes, good looking. She was brought here 9 months ago by a Mr. Zunts from Mobile.

28 Oct 1846. $10 Reward. Ran away the 18th, a black boy, WILLIAM (calls himself JOHN when absent), 21, 5' 11", 175 pounds. Good looks and fine form. WILLIAM BLEAKLEY.

31 Oct 1846. $500 Reward. Ran away my man DENNIS, a mulatto, 24, 5' 6", can read and perhaps can write. He is a house servant and has worked on board stamaboats. SEABORN TRAVIS, Mobile.

1 Nov 1846. $20 Reward. Ran away the 29th ult. the mulatto man SAM, about 6' high, 200 lbs. Has a large scar on one hand, is a baker by trade. DAVID BARBOUR.

4 Nov 1846. $20 Reward for apprehension of my boy MIKE, who ran away yesterday. He is a very likely boy, aged 22, about 5' 10", active and intelligent; dresses genteel, having been raised as a body servant. E. L. YANCEY.

6 Nov 1846. Stolen about the 8th of March last year near Lake Providence, a black boy named LEWIS, alias TOM, 27, common size, a scar on his mouth. T. R. McCLINTOCK.

6 Nov 1846. $10 Reward. Ran away the 4th inst. a negro boy about 40, 5' 10", dark griff color, a scar on his forehead. He is a tailor by trade and is known as BENNETT or BARNET JOHNSON. D. WHEELER.

12 Nov 1846. $5 Reward for the black boy SAM who ran away 3 weeks ago. He is about 19, about 6' tall, very slim. Was purchased of Mr. Genois who keeps the brickyard. HENRY SCHRODER.

18 Nov 1846. $25 Reward will be paid for apprehension of a negro man named EDMOND, 21, a bright mulatto, 5' 9". Says he once belonged to Mrs. Shall and to Charles Lynch of this city. He left one of the Vicksburg packets about 3 weeks ago while in New Orleans. A. J. GILLESPIE.

26 Nov 1846. $10 Reward. Ran away the 9th, a negro girl named ADALINE, 20, about 5' 2", thick lips, large eyes and a large scar on one of her breasts. MARY KIRK.

6 Dec 1846. $20 Reward. Ran away the negro man PRINCE, alias FRANK, who formerly belonged to Mr. Rousseau; 5' 6", jet black complexion, good teeth. Very intelligent. Mrs. THOMAS HILL.

12 Dec 1846. $10 Reward for the negro woman CELESTE, aged 50, middle size, black skin, one front tooth missing. She ran away last August. R. CASTANADE.

16 Dec 1846. $20 Reward. Ran away Wednesday on his way down in the steamer Prairie Bird, between Plaquemine and Donaldsonville, the yellow boy GEORGE, 26, 5' 10", keen looking. M. METCALF, Natchez.

16 Dec 1846. $20 Reward. Will be given for arrest of the negro boy RICHARD, about 32, 5' 10", very broken teeth. C. MOORE.

2 Jan 1847. $20 Reward. Ran away in December the griff boy ISAM, 23, 5' 2", speaks quick. ROBERT ALLEN.

6 Jan 1847. $10 Reward. Ran away the 2d inst. a negro woman named CELIA, about 36, of yellow complexion, formerly belonged to Mrs. Drake. T. RAY.

8 Jan 1847. $100 reward will be paid to any person who will return to me the negro girl EUGENIA and her mulatto child, aged 2 years. She was enticed away by her former owner, Madam Widow Decaux in December. J. B. DUPEIRE.

12 Jan 1847. $20 Reward. Ran away the negro man GEORGE, alias BROWN, formerly belonging to Ulysee Frehan of this city. He is of yellow complexion, about 37, 5' 8", a blacksmith by trade. He has run as a fireman on the steamboat Clinton. His wife is at Mr. Frehan's. He speaks French and English. W. T. BROWN.

13 Jan 1847. $15 Reward. Ran away the 8th inst. a negro man called WILEY, dark griff complexion, 25, 6' tall. He was lately purchased of Mr. Davis, a trader. SAMUEL McFARMER.

17 Jan 1847 $10 Reward will be given for apprehension of the mulatto girl (quarteroon) HANNAH, 20, ordinary size, aged 20; speaks English and German. L. BOULIGNY, Lafayette.

22 Jan 1847. $20 Reward will be paid for arrest of the quarteroon girl named HANNA JOHNSON, 20, bright color, straight black hair, 20 years old. She was purchased from Col. J. R. White of this city in Dec. 1845, who brought her here from St. Louis, Mo. She left in December. L. BOULIGNY, Lafayette.

2 Feb 1847. $10 Reward will be given for apprehension of the negro woman SARAH, 31, 5' 2", stout built, speaks French, English, and Spanish. JOSE A. LANONDO.

8 Feb 1847. $10 Reward. Left the steamboat Little Rock on Monday morning, the mulatto boy named BOB MALANE, 40, 5' 4". WILLIAM ARNOLD.

8 Feb 1847. $10 Reward. Ran away from Mrs. Shall, Canal st., the 6th inst. the negro girl ELBA, 16, small size, very black, handsome face. RICHARD KING.

10 Feb 1847. Ran away from my plantation, 84 miles above New Orleans, the mulatto man named ROBERT ALEXANDER, 35, 5' 10", stout built. He left last December.

13 Feb 1847. $25 Reward will be paid for the yellow boy IRVIN, who belongs to Mr. Nathaniel Pickett, of Red River, very light color and might pass for white. He is 18 years old, about 5' 7" tall.

20 Feb 1847. $200 Reward. Left on the 10th inst. the griffe boy JOHN JOSEPH, 32, 5' 5", well built, fine teeth, speaks French and English. I bought him from Ephraim Adam Carter of Memphis. He had his left leg burnt in the explosion of a boiler on a steamboat and wears a wooden leg at the knee joint. A. MARCHESSAU.

24 Feb 1847. $5 Reward. Ran away the negro woman SOPHY, 46, 5' 6", speaks French and English. She originally had 6 fingers on each hand, but had the 6th ones cut off. She wears card #1121. AMELIA RYMON.

24 Feb 1847. $10 Reward will be paid for the arrest of the slave GEORGE, a brickmaker by trade, belonging to M. E. LAMBREMONT, of Bayou Goula. He formerly belonged to Mr. Rayon of this city. He left the 15th inst. D. FROSELAIZS.

25 Feb 1847. $10 Reward. Ran away the 20th, my negress THISBY, 25, dark griff color, very fleshy. G. B. MASON.

27 Feb 1847. $10 Reward. Ran away from his mistress 22 Feb. in Mobile, the dark quarteroon boy CHARLES or WILLIAM, 17, speaks English and a little French.

2 Mar 1847. $10 Reward. Ran away the 11th, ult. the griff girl EPHEMY THOMAS, nicknamed "Feme". She is rather stout, of middle size, speaks English only, and is about 26 years old.

7 Mar 1847. $400 Reward. Will be paid for the boy WASHINGTON, who ran away 23 Nov. 1846. He is 40, about 5' 9", is marked by the smallpox. Formerly belonged to John Freeland. H. FASSMAN.

13 Mar 1847. Ran away 19 Feb. CHARLOTTE, rather black, about 33, 4' 5". The number of her medal is 1901. A liberal reward will be paid for her return. Mrs. M. MURRAY.

14 Mar 1847. $10 Reward. Ran away the 12th inst. the negro girl MARTHA, 20, 5' 6", good looking, well formed. GEORGE W. JONES.

21 Mar 1847. $10 Reward. Absconded the 17th, the negro boy JERRY, 22 belonging to NEILY BRENT. Had with him a brass badge, #2026. J. GLOVER.

21 Mar 1847. Absconded from my plantation at Racourei Bend, Pointe Coupee Parish, the following slaves: JACK, 30, rather dark. JEFFER, 23, large and strong. PHILIP, 23. MINOR, 28, very light complexion. RUBEN, 28, not very dark. TOM, 20. HENRY, 20, tall and slim. MOSES and MARY (no description). A. LEDOUX.

26 Mar 1847. $50 Reward will be paid for the slave BETSY, 4' 7", who absconded last April. She speaks French and English. Two fingers of the left hand are off at the first joint. JOHN NEWBERRY.

27 Mar 1847. $20 Reward for JOE, 14, 5' 2", formerly belonging to Mr. John Freeland.

27 Mar 1847. $20 Reward will be paid for SUSAN, 13 years old, very light color, and would pass for white. Dark hazel eyes, straight hair and is a hair dresser by trade. Speaks English only. ANN JOHNSON.

27 Mar 1847. $25 reward will be paid for apprehension of my negro boy, BOB, who absconded 19 March; black complexion, 15 years old, took with him brass badge #799. ISAAC PIPKIN.

30 Mar 1847. $100 reward will be paid for apprehension of the negro man FRANK, 5' 9", 18 years old. I purchased him from James Elder of New Orleans last December. He ran away from my plantation at Pointe Coupee 6 months ago. He is of a dark griffe color. ASA BROWN.

1 Apr 1847. $25 Reward. Ran away a dark mulatto girl named MILLY, 17, 5' 2", formerly belonged to Mrs. S. Dixon. R. W. ELRICH.

9 Apr 1847. $50 reward. Ran away from Vicksburg, Miss., on the 3d inst. a negro man named SIMON, who I bought from John S. Smith of Charleston, S. C. He is about 24, dark complexion, weighs about 165 pounds. JAMES L. POWERS.

13 Apr 1847. $20 Reward. Ran away the 11 inst. from Harlem Plantation, parish of Plaquemines, 38 miles below the city, the negro slave SAM TAYLOR, 5' 9", 38 years old.

14 Apr 1847. $20 Reward. Ran away the light black boy JOHN WHITE, 5' 6", bow-legged. Formerly drove a bread cart in the city. We bought him from Mr. Chappotin who bought him from S. N. Hite last year. He had on an iron collar. D'AQUIN BROTHERS.

14 Apr 1847. $50 Reward. Ran away from Vicksburg, Miss., on 3 April, a negro called SIMON, property of John S. Smith, late of Charleston, S.C. He is 5' 9", weighs 170 lbs. and is about 24. JAMES L. POWERS.

14 Apr 1847. $100 reward will be paid for the negro FRANK, purchased by me from James Elder in New Orleans last December. He ran off from my plantation, parish of Pointe Coupee, right after being bought. He is a dark griff, about 5' 9", 18 years old. ASA BROWN.

14 Apr 1847. $50 Reward. Ran away last February a negro woman named CHRISTINE, aged 55, about 5' 6", speaks French and broken English. GEORGE SWENEY.

15 Apr 1847. $10 Reward. Ran away a creole named HENRY or HARRY, about 5' 4", aged 20, curly hair, speaks French and English. D'AQUIN BROTHERS.

15 Apr 1847. The griffe girl HARRIET ran away on the 9th. She is about 28, 5' 3", a scar on her forehead, speaks French, English and Spanish. Apply the Picayune.

15 Apr 1847. $50 Reward will be paid for LOUISA, who ran off the 8th inst. She is 5' 7", 24. She was purchased in Louisville. Steamboat captains are warned not to harbor her. JOHN WHITE.

15 Apr 1847. $50 Reward. Ran away from the steamer Fashion, in the port of New Orleans, about 14 days ago my negro boy FESTUS, a mulatto, 5' 8", 23, humble deportment. Formerly belonged to John G. Banks of New Orleans. WILLIAM F. ROBERTSON, Terrebone Parish.

23 Apr 1847. $100 reward will be paid for the boys BEN and SANA. Ben is about 22, speaks French and English. Sana is about 17, has long curly hair, speaks French but little English. WIDOW N. BOUNY.

25 Apr 1847. $10 will be paid for arrest of the boy JACK, who belongs to Lieut. Albert H. Rippetoe, of Talledega Co, Ala., of the 1st Regiment of Alabama Volunteers, now in Mexico. He was with his master in Mexico for 10 months, and ran away between Mexico and Alabama, where he was sent by his master. He is about 23, weighs 165 lbs. and is about 5' 9".

25 Apr 1847. $10 reward will be paid for the negro boy TOBY, who ran away yesterday. He was a fireman for last 2 years on the steamer Fashion. He is about 24, 5' 2" tall.

25 Apr 1847. $20 Reward. Ran away from Madam Shawl on Friday a mulatto girl named AMANDA, 5' 4", 20, and far advanced in pregnancy. She was purchased from S. M. Haggerty in Louisville, Ky., and raised there.

29 Apr 1847. $10 Reward. Ran away the griff boy JOHN, owned by Joseph N. Batson. He is 5' 6", 35, and works as a stevedore on ships and steamboats.

30 Apr 1847. $100 reward. Ran away in March the dark mulatto boy LEWIS, 15, a good waiter. He was brought from Charleston, S.C., to New Orleans and has lived in Florida. I bought him in December, 1845, from Hiram Nansen. A. B. JAMES.

1 May 1847. $10 Reward. Ran away the 25th ultimo, the negro boy EDWARD, 5' 11", 22 years old. WILLIAM N. BATSON.

2 May 1847. $75 Reward. Left my plantation on False River, April 25, 3 negro men. CALLOWAY, 5' 7", LEWIS, 5' 7", and SAM, 5' 7". I bought them in New Orleans from E. E. Powell. R. G. STERLING.

9 May 1847. $50 Reward. Ran away 20 April the mulatto slave VIRGILE, 16. He formerly belonged to Louise Hardouine. CHARLES LAMARQUE.

25 May 1847. $20 Reward. Ran away from Lafayette, La., on the 19th, the slave MOSES, 5' 7", 46 years old. Formerly belonged to J. B. Conger, in Mississippi. A. F. JONES.

26 May 1847. $25 Reward. Ran away the 19th, a griffe woman named ROMAINE, 5' tall, about 25, slender, and has lost one of her big toes. T. P. KOSTMAYER.

5 Jun 1847. $100 Reward. Ran away from the steamboat Bois d'Arc on 12 May a dark mulatto named BILL MISSOURI, about 25. He was purchased from Henry Moore, Boonville, Mo., last December. JOHN H. GORDON.

10 Jun 1847. $100 Reward will be paid for delivery of the negro boy DENIS, 5' 5", 25, dark complexion, lame in one leg. He left Lafayette on Saturday. He came from Osceola, Ark., 10 days ago with WILLIAM BARD, his owner.

16 Jun 1847. $100 Reward. Ran away on the 12th, the negro man HENRY SIPP, about 20, has a limp, and is very black. He had on Badge #788. Also, BOB, 16, black, had on Badge #799. ISAAC PIPKIN.

27 Jun 1847. Left on the 2d inst. 2 mulatto slaves, SAM and NELSON. Sam is about 30, 200 lbs., 6' tall. Nelson is about

23, 5' 7", lately from Mobile. They are both bakers. DAVID BARBOUR.

1 Jul 1847. $10 Reward. Ran away the 27th of June a mulatto boy named WILLIAM SPINK, 5' 7", 21. Has a ring in one of his ears. He is a Creole and speaks French and English. ALEXANDER PHILLIPS.

11 Jul 1847. $20 Reward. The strong and stout mulatto HENRY MACKEY ran away on 28 June from Jefferson parish. He is about 5' 7", aged 30. He was bought in December from B. W. Powell of Kentucky. N. N. DESTREHAN.

16 Jul 1847. $50 reward will be paid for ISAAC, who ran away in March. He is a mulatto, about 25, a white spot on his forehead. Limps slightly. He was raised in new Orleans and is a brick-mason by trade. IRA SMITH.

24 Jul 1847. $20 Reward. Ran away the yellow boy HENRY, 22, 5' 8", formerly belonged to Miss M. Raymond. Has been on board steamboats as cook and steward. He had irons and chains on his legs. W. N. ROGERS.

27 Jul 1847. $100 Reward. Ran away the 24th: BEN, 14, slim built, dark griffe color, was bought last June from Daniel G. Kiger of Washington Co., Texas. THOMAS C. MALONE.

27 Jul 1847. Ran away from my plantation in Sabine parish, 25 miles from Natchitoches 4 slaves: MINGO, 26, 5', a scar on one knee made by a knife. ABRAM, 23, 5', a scar over one eye made by a broad axe. TONY, 5' 9", 18. BEN, 5' 4", 19 lame in one leg. All are black. JAMES S. MURPHY.

3 Aug 1847. $20 Reward. Ran away the 27th ultimo a griff man BILL, 5' 10", 30, some front teeth out, two fingers off the left hand. He is a cook by trade and has run on the river on different boats. JAMES H. ADAMS.

8 Aug 1847. $10 reward will be paid for a black man named PETER who left on the 4th, with an iron collar around his neck. He formerly belonged to James Dunn of New Orleans. MAX BLOCK.

8 Aug 1847. $10 Reward. Ran away the 25th of last month, the negro PAUL, 33, black, stout, lame in his left leg, has been a bricklayer's helper.

8 Aug 1847. $20 Reward. Ran away from the plantation of R. C. Camp on the 24th ult., 2 negro men, BYRON and CHARLES. Byron is about 55, an African, speaks bad English. He wears a truss for a rupture, and is about 5' 6". Charles is about 5' 8", not very dark, has many stripes of the lash. I will give $10 for each of them. ROBERT C. CAMP.

8 Aug 1847. $20 Reward. Ran away on 25 June a negro named JOHNSON, about 30 and 5' tall. He is little bald, of dark complexion, upper jaw front teeth missing. He is generally known by the name, Star Johnson, and has been long employed as a carriage driver. His former master was the late Mr. Rowling.

8 Aug 1847. $25 Reward. Ran away 25 July the griff boy JOE, 5' 5", 19, speaks French and English. He was raised by H. W. PALFREY and more recently owned by John Freeland. ORRAN BYRD.

10 Aug 1847. $5 Reward. Ran away 1 May the mulattress SARAH, stout built, long straight hair. She belonged to the

late CYRUS BRADLEY a few years ago. She is an excellent washer and ironer.

10 Aug 1847. $10 Reward. Ran away in Lafayette the slave ANDREW, 5' 10", very black. Teeth somewhat decayed. CHARLES R. KENNEDY.

13 Aug 1847. $20 Reward. Ran away from the plantation of Robert A. Wilkinson, 40 miles below the city on the 8th inst. the griff WASHINGTON, 5' 11", aged 30. He was purchased of Mrs. M. B. Carter of Bayou Sara.

13 Aug 1847. $20 reward will be paid for arrest of a negro man named LEVI, a dark mulatto, 180 lbs., bow-legged. He ran away from Macon, Ga., on 11 July. H. L. COOK, Macon, Ga.

1 Sep 1847. $50 reward will be paid for the mulatto EDMOND, who ran away on July 24. He is very stout, 5' 2". He plays the clarionet at colored balls and parties and has a license from the state of Louisiana to sell as a peddler. He was a drummer for some years in one of the military companies in New Orleans. For the past 18 months he was a seller of ready made clothes. PAUL ALDIGE.

2 Sep 1847. $10 Reward for the negro man ELIJAH, 5' 5", aged 50, who ran away Aug. 15 from Wilmington, N. C. He is a cooper by trade. JOHN HALL.

2 Sep 1847. $10 Reward. Absconded from me 2 days ago the dark mulatto girl named MIYADLINE, 23, 5' 5", good teeth. She sold milk in Lafayette. J. P. PHILLIPS.

2 Sep 1847. $20 Reward. Ran away 20 Aug. the mulatto boy DICK, 5' 9", 23, freckles on his hands and face. He was purchased from James Kirman. OLIVER DUBOIS.

5 Sep 1847. $30 Reward. Ran away from the schooner Martha, on 25 July the copper colored boy BRAZILE, 18, about 5' 7". He was purchased from George A. Botts in June. JOHN HURLEY.

5 Sep 1847. $10 reward for CRESSY, a black, 5' 7", 56 years old. Was formerly owned in Mobile by Mrs. Doyle who brought her to New Orleans. JOHN KEAN.

5 Sep 1847. $50 Reward. Ran away November 20, 1846, near Plaquemine, Iberville parish, a negro boy named SANDY. He is of black complexion, 5' 6", about 130 lbs. Speaks French and English, walks lame, shows marks of whips on his back and thighs. W. H. CARR.

11 Sep 1847. $75 Reward will be paid for arrest of the yellow boy JIM CARR, a carpenter by trade, about 5' 9", 28 years old. He left July 2. Was formerly owned by Henry E. Moore, Boonville, Mo.

16 Sep 1847. $20 reward will be paid for arrest of my negro man JOHN BAPTISTE, who left my plantation last March. He is of light complexion, 5' 9", 50 years old. On examination he will be found to have been severely whipped. I purchased him 2 years ago from Thomas Johnson of Cape Girardeau, Mo., where he was raised. AUGUSTIN PUGH.

16 Sep 1847. $20 reward for a negro man HENRY or HARRY who left me on the 10th. He is 26 years old, is a creole negro, speaks French and English. Formerly belonged to Ferdinand Le Most. JAMES PHILLIPS.

23 Sep 1847. $20 reward will be paid for the mulatto boy JAMES JOHNSON, 5' 7". He can read, write and speak English. WILLIAM WEBB.

23 Sep 1847. $10 Reward. Ran away the 14th inst. a negro boy named CUPID, about 27, a scar under the left eye. DOMINIC PIQUESNI.

23 Sep 1847. $10 Reward. Ran away, the boy HERCULES or CAESAR, who came here from Charleston, S.C., in July. He is about 20, 5' 4" tall, speaks only English.

24 Sep 1847. $20 Reward. Ran away 21st inst. JANE, 25, griff color, no front teeth, about 5' 6" tall. She was decoyed off by her husband, John, a griff colored man belonging to Capt. Wendell. D. A. HARRIS.

25 Sep 1847. $50 Reward. Ran away 20th inst. the slave HENRY, 5' 7", aged 31, light griff complexion, a ship caulker by trade. He was brought to New Orleans last November from Alexandria, D. C. S. V. BURTON, Algiers, La.

10 Oct 1847. Absconded from my plantation in DeSoto parish a mulatto man named HENRY, 30 years old, straight hair, a blacksmith by trade. He worked several years on the Charleston railroad. I purchased him from a Mr. Martin of Attala Co., Miss. JOHN A. GAMBLE, Grand Cane, La.

29 Oct 1847. $25 Reward. Will be paid for my negro boy STEPHEN, 5' 8", blue eyes, light hair, complexion almost white. He sometimes goes by the names of STEPHEN SMITH and GEORGE SMITH. LEWIS PERANA.

5 Nov 1847. $10 Reward. Absented himself Wednesday, the griff boy ELI, 19 years old, 5' 6", has been a cab driver for the past 2 years. He had an iron collar around his neck when he left. JOHN McLEGGAN.

5 Nov 1847. $150 Reward. Ran away from the plantation of H. J. Grover, parish of West Baton Rouge, about 20 March last, 2 negro men: ISOM, 40, 5' 6". Is in the habit of running away and has marks of the whip; and BILL, 25, 5' 6", a scar across his forehead.

17 Nov 1847. $20 Reward. Ran away from me living near Delta, Coshoma Co., Miss., on the 20th of August, a negro boy named PETER. He is of dark color, weighs 125 lbs., is about 24. His speech assimilates closely that of the Guinea tribe. AARON SHELBY.

15 Dec 1847. $5 Reward. Ran away the 8th instant the negro woman PAMELLA, aged 36, about 5' tall. Has 6 fingers on each hand. Speaks French and English. J. N. GLAUDIN.

16 Dec 1847. $50 Reward will be paid for delivery of the State slave CHARLES HILL, who left the Esperance plantation in St. John the Baptist parish the 7th instant. He is an excellent blacksmith and an engineer. He was purchased in April in New Orleans from G. M. Davis who purchased him from J. M. Reynolds of Natchez, Miss., where he left a wife and children.

27 Dec 1847. $50 Reward. Ran away from the steamboat Missouri on the 17th, 2 negro men, WILLIAM, light black, 28, 5' 7", and JERRY, black, 26, 5' 10". T. C. TWITCHELL.

23 Dec 1847. $20 reward will be paid to whoever will deliver to me the mulatto, ST. JEAN. He is tall and slender, about 20

years old. He was raised by his former owner, Mr. Tremoulet. V. DAVID.

26 Dec 1847. $25 Reward. Ran away a month ago the negro boy named MAY. He is about 5' 6", 25 years old. He came to New Orleans from Charleston, S. C. H. GILLY.

26 Dec 1847. $20 Reward. Will be paid for arrest of the negro boy CHANCE, alias JACOB, about 38 years old, about 5' 4" tall. He has a slight limp, and scars on his face from dog bites. He was formerly owned by W. J. Andrews of New Orleans. JAMES BRADFORD, Pascagoula, Miss.

Index
Slaveholders and Others

ABERNATHY, Hanna & Kirkman 47
ADAMS & McCall 109
ADAMS, James H. 122
AICARD, Mr. 35
AITKENS, John S. 91
ALCORN, James L. 40
ALDIGE, Paul 123
ALLEN, C. J. 102 Charles 75 J. D. 106 Robert 113
AMELUNG, Mr. 54
ANDERS, M. G. 98
ANDERSON, Larkin M. 20 William J. 60
ANDREWS, J. 36 W. J. 127
ANTHONY, G. B. 96
ARMAT, Thomas 11
ARNOLD, William 114
ATKINSON, Major 94
AUGUSTIN, D. 88
AUSTEN, R. M. 101
AVARD, Mr. 30
AVERY, William H. 11 44

BAGGETT, B. 34
BAGLEY, David T. 78
BAILEY, J. A. 29
BAKUP, B. A. 51
BALDWIN, Mordecai 27
BANKS, John G. 118
BARBAY, Mrs. 104
BARBOUR, David 28 52 79 112 121
BARBRE, Jose 56
BARD, William 120
BARKER, Jacob 18
BARKLEY, William 12
BARNES, G. W. 80
BARNEY, Mrs. 95
BATSON, Joseph N. 119 William N. 119
BATTISTE, John 33
BATY, Mr. 18
BAUDARD, Thomas 99
BAUM, Sarah 31
BAXTER, H. V. 8
BAYLISS, Mr. 105
BEARD, G. R. 102 George A. 71 J. A. 29 45 51 63-65 73 77 81 87 107 Joseph A. 36 Mr. 25
BEASLY, John C. 9
BEHAN & Mitchell 62
BELL, Hugh 74 Samuel 35 58 88 98 W. W. 87 William 76
BELLE, Mlle. 69
BEN, Jacob 59
BENNETT & Fager 91
BENNETT, S. 3 W. A. 104
BERRY, James M. 50
BERTRAND, John 28
BIENVENU, F. M. 90

BILHARTZ, Anthony 64
BIRD, Mr. 32
BLACK, Alexander 62
   Hambright 10
BLAKE, A. 84
BLAKENY, James T. 99
BLANC, E. 74 Evariste 87
   Jules A. 40 94
BLANCHARD, Mr. 26 53 61
BLEAKLEY, William
   110-111
BLEASOE, D. H. 21
BLISS, O. A. 93
BLOCK, Max 122
BLOOM, August 94
BODARD, Mr. 48
BOGEAURD, Judge 98
BOTTS, George A. 5 13 16
   40 44 46 84 93 96 99
   124
BOUDAR, Thomas 101
BOUDOUSQUIE, Antoine
   93
BOULIGNY, L. 114 M. 91
   Mr. 18 U. Jr. 70
BOULWARE, A. 99
BOUNY, Widow N. 119
BOWE & Crenshaw 59
BOWIE, R. P. 21 Reason 34
BOYKIN & Noriss 11
BRABSTON, James M. 111
BRACKENRIDGE, Mr. 19
BRADFORD, James 127
   Mabachia 81
BRADLEY, Cyrus 123
   Henry 36 Sarah Ann 82

BRADY, Mr. 8
BRAUD, J. A. 72 85 97 109
BRENT, Neily 116
BRISKEY, Mr. 18
BROTHERS, D'Aquin 10 79
   104 117-118 Freret 26 92
BROWN, Asa 117-118
   Clement 104 J. N. 50
   James 24 Miss. James
   Senr. 54 W. T. 114
BROWNLEE, James 87
BRYAN, Mr. 20
BUFFET, J. F. 71
BUILLIT, Cuthbert 74
BULLER, John 16
BURTON, S. V. 125
BUTLER 27 Judge 28 Mr. 20
   William 83
BYRD, Orran 57 90 122
BYRNE, Gregory 44 46 J. B.
   72 John B. 50
BYRNES, J. B. 64

CALDWELL, James H. 17
CALDWELL, L. A. 4 14 64
   85 95 Lucy 50
CAMP, R. C. 122 Robert C.
   122
CAMPBELL & Labranche 97
CAMPBELL, Mr. 64 William
   80
CANTRELL, Mr. 69
CANTRELLE, Mr. 18
CARNES & Tate 98
CARR, W. H. 124
CARRICO, George 19

CARSON, Joseph B. 38-39
CARTER, Dr. 79
CARTER, E. C. 95 Edward
   C. 86 Ephraim Adam
   115 H. N. 53 James 102
   Mr. 28 Mrs. 6 Mrs. M.
   B. 123
CASTANADE, R. 113
CAVALLIER Theofile 32
CHALMERS, John G. 39
CHANDLER, Mr. 15
CHAPPOTIN, Mr. 117
CHARBONNET, A. E. 23
CHARLES, Richard 81 95
CHIAPPEL, C. 25
CHOUTEAU, Mr. 63
CHRISTIAN, Mr. 26
CHURCHILL, C. W. 39 Mr. 34
COCHRAN, Edward 96 John 85 Mr. 103
COFFEY, Charles 106
COGSWELL, E. B. 7
COHEN, Aaron 79
COLBERT, Vicy 16
COLHOUN, Gustavos 101
COLLAGIANI, P. 22
COLLERTON, William 9
COLLETT, Joseph 69
COLLINS, J. W. 32
COMPTON, William H. 4
CONGER, J. B. 120
CONLIN, Mr. 73
CONNER, Mr. 23
CONREY, Peter 15
CONWAY, James R. 23

COOK, H. L. 123
COPMAN, Henry 85
CORLIS, James 22
CORNU, B. 111
COSTE, Mr. 38
COTTLE, John 13
COULTER, S. H. 8
COWAN, Jesse 62
COX, Isabella 60
COYLE, James 62
CRANE, Mr. 16 William 46
CREON, John 26
CRINE, C. 107
CROCKETT, J. S. 42
CROISI, Mr. 39
CROSS, Benjamin 13 111
CRUZAT, M. 57
CURRIE, John 77
CUVILLER, Mr. 35
CZARNOWSKE, H. 37

D. POINCY & Co. 106
DALE, Mr. 28
DALTON, Dr. 9 21
DALY, Peter 92
DAVEZAC, Dr. 85
DAVID, John S. 111 V. 127
DAVIDSON, T. G. 91
DAVIS 49 G. M. 126 George 109 J. Jr. 8 103 110 Mack 104 Mark 65 82 Mr. 30 114 Thomas T. 59
DAYAL, Henry 65
DAYTON, Mrs. D. 96
DE PASS, Samuel 100

DECAUX, Madame Widow 113
DELERIE, Mr. 24 30
DELONY, Batiste 35
DEROU, Jean 108
DESFORGES, A. 52
DESTREHAN, N. N. 121
DEVEREAUX, M. H. 20
DIAMOND, Charles 29 40
DICKEY, Mr. 15
DIGGES, J. B. 18 Major 63-64
DIGGS, James B. 9
DIXON, James 14 Mrs. S. 117 S. D. 1
DOBB, Mr. 38
DOLI, Mendelin 70
DONALSON, A. H. 102
DORE, John 109
DOUGHERTY & Co. 12
DOWDY, Mr. 34
DOWNEY, R. T. 64
DOWTY, Z. 110
DOYLE & May 7
DOYLE, Mrs. 124 Peter 61
DRAKE, B. P. 72 Mrs. 113 W. T. 51
DRUILKET, Jules 102
DRUMMOND, J. 61
DUBOIS, Oliver 124 Pierre 35
DUBORD, P. A. 106 108
DUBUISE, Pierre 18
DUBUQUE, Mr. 34
DUBUYS, Adelle 15
DUFILHO, H. 77

DUGGAN, John 37
DUNN, James 122
DUPARC Brothers & Locoul 81
DUPEIRE, J. B. 113
DUPLANTIER, Madame Fergus 109
DUPLESSIS, V. 57
DURKER, H. J. 73
DUVALL, Mr. 38

EATON, B. C. 39
EDY, Mr. 20
EGAN, Mr. 34 Owen D. 39
ELDER, James 117
ELLIOTT, R. W. 27
ELLMAKER & Shropshire 97
ELRICH, R. W. 117
ENSIGN, Mr. 85
ERWIN, A. 43
ESINAR, Mr. 18
EUSINE, Mr. 19
EVANS, James 4

FAGOT, Samuel 78
FAITH, J. W. 49
FASSMAN, H. 116
FAZENDE, F. E. 25
FEHRMAN, D. 18
FERGUSON, E. C. 104
FERNANDEZ, Anthony 67 75
FERRIS, Henry 67 102
FETTINGTON, R. 104
FIELD, O. K. 101 Seaman 90

FISK, F. M. 43
FLAGG, George 41
FLEISCHMAN, D. 70
FLEISCHMANN, D. 58
FLYNN, P. 60
FOLEY, A. M. 99
FOLSE, Edward 13
FONTEROY, Mr. 38
FORBUSH, A. E. 36
FORRESTE, Mr. 38
FORSYTH, G. C. 64
FORT, W. A. 28
FORTIER, Arthur 107 Mr. 26
FOURCHI, Mr. 26
FOX, J. 38 71 80 Madam 45
FREDERICK, Augustin 47
FREELAND, John 116 122
FREEMAN, Theophile 44 48
FREHAN, Ulysee 114
FRETWELL, Mrs. 43
FROSELAIZS, D. 115
FROST, W. J. 12

GAMBLE, John A. 125
GAMBLINZ, Miles 62
GANDET, D. 104 Valry 104
GANT, George W. 48
GARDNER, E. J. 107
GARNER, Wilford 34
GARRET, James 2
GARRISON, Mr. 23
GAUNAULT, S. 60
GENOIR, C. 26
GENOIS, Mr. 112
GEORGE, Alexander 81 89 94 G. W. 77

GERNON, Peter 28
GILLESPIE, A. J. 112
GILLY, H. 127
GLAUDIN, J. N. 126 John N. 74
GLAZE, P. H. 104
GLIDDEN, John S. 105
GLOVER, Capt. 19 J. 116
GLYNN, Charles R. 12
GONZALEZ, Francis 71
GOODRICH, C. 49 William C. 47
GORDON, John H. 120
GORIN & Smith 107
GRADY, Mr. 103
GRAY, Martha 10
GRAYSON, John B. 83
GREEN & McDougall 108
GREEN, Daniel 39 John U. 16
GREENE, John 65 Mr. 31
GREEVES, John G. 89
GREGORY, D. S. 31 Mr. 53
GRIFFIN, Isham 7
GROSJEAN, Mr. 24
GROVER, H. J. 126
GUERIN, Madame Edouard 101
GUISHONNET, J. 87
GUIYOM, Tousaint 6
GUSTAFFE, Mr. 35

HAGAN, J. 90
HAGGERTY, S. M. 119
HAGGETT, T. 60
HAINES & Co. 66

HALL, J. 7 John 21 123
William 57
HALPHEN, Mrs. Widow 88
HALSEY, Dr. 88
HAMBLEN, S. 61
HAND, John H. 76 85
HANNA, James J. 53 Mrs. 59
Sarah 53 55
HANSON, P. 102
HARDOUINE, Louise 120
HARMAN, Mr. 20
HARPER, H. S. 16 18
HARRALL, John 105
HARRIS, Alex 98 Capt. 13
D. A. 125 William 62
HARRISON, Jesse 41
HARRISON, William 97
HART, Jesse 48 56 84 89
HARTY, Philip 14
HATCH, F. H. 69 78 N. T. 23
N. W. 26
HAWKINS, Mr. 59 Napoleon
B. 86
HAWLEY, Madame 43
HAYDEL, M. B. 90
HAYDEN, Felix 15
HAYES, U. C. E. 24
HEINE, John 37
HENDERSON, William 75
HENETTY, Bridget 27
HENRY, Benjamin 42
HESS, Leonard 58
HICKEY, Mr. 25
HIGGINS 24
HIGH, Solomon 107

HILL, Mrs. Thomas 113 O.
B. 40
HINGHAM, A. B. 84
HITE, Mr. 20 S. N. 12 64 117
HOEY, John 43
HOFFMAN, Mr. 102
HOLLIDAY, James 45-46
HOLLOWAY, H. W. 50
HOLMES, Willis 72
HOPKINS & Nugent 54
HOPKINS, Mr. 30
HOSMER, Mary J. 55
HOWARD, J. H. 62 P. 31
HOWTELL, Robert 52
HUEY, Mr. 46
HUGHES, Mr. 29
HUMPHREY, Alex 56
HUMPHREYS, Mr. 19
HUNDLEY, Thomas 47
HUNT, Wilkins 52
HUNTINGTON, B. W. 105
H. A. 70
HURLEY, John 124
HUTCHINS, Capt. 63 67
HUTTON, Isabel M. 76
HYAMS, H. M. 17
HYDE, John E. 55 83 L. D. 13
HYNOR, Lewis 71

IRVIN, Miller 37
IRWIN, Hall & Walton 3
ISSACS, William 34

JACOBS, Charles A. 35 64
JAMES, A. B. 119 Mr. 20 59

JANE, Mary 37
JAQUES, George 89
JARDELL, Marguéretta 40
JARRELL, William 59
JAULLE, Mr. 31
JENKINS, James 100 Leon 23
JOHNSON, Ann 117 Isham 61 Madame 36 Mr. 33 Sherman 5 Stephen 4 Thomas 124 Thomas J. 79 William 39 54 79
JOHNSTON, E. 43 George S. 3 P. 7
JONES & Turner 3
JONES, A. F. 120 George W. 116 John S. 59 L. 3 Lawrence 6 M.. P. 53 William 103
JORDAN, L. W. 10
JULIEN, Mr. 19
JUMONVILLE, C. 98 100

KATZENBERGER, Christian 100
KEAFFE, John 63
KEAN, John 124
KELLER, George 45 John 31
KELLOGG, John Jay 30
KELLY, E. B. 2
KELVIT, Mr. 16
KENDIG, Benjamin 15 21 66
KENNEDY, C. H. 31 Charles R. 123 Mrs. 100 T. 69
KENNER, W. B. 99
KENT, R. A. 75

KERNER, Charles 40
KERR, Mr. 22 Mrs. 71
KIGER, Daniel G. 121
KING, Richard 73 114
KIRK, George G. 106 Mary 113
KIRMAN, James 124
KOCK, Charles 89
KOSTMAYER, T. P. 120
KRESS, Joseph 52
KRISBERGER, Caspar 41
KRITZBERGER, K. 38

LA Branch, Judge 105
LABRANCHE, Drausia 32 Lucian 70 Lucien 89 104
LABROUCHE, Mr. 51
LACOSTE, Mr. 19
LAFORE, Mr. 18
LAGORY, Auguste 91
LAMARQUE, C. 60 Charles 120
LAMBERT, L. 102 Mr. 24
LAMBETH, W. M. 46 76
LAMBREMONT, M. E. 115
LAMKIN, John 93 John T. 92
LANE, J. W. 75 N. C. 16
LANIER, Thomas J. 10
LANONDO, Jose A. 114
LAPISSE, Mr. 18
LAPPALIT, Mr. 37
LARAN, Mr. 28
LATAPIE, J. T. 23
LAUDUN, Henry 37
LAVASELLE, Mr. 18

LAYET, Adolphe 57 P. E. 66
LAYTON, Mrs. 69
LAZARUS, Isaac 6
LE CESNE, J. 96
LE MOST, Ferdinand 124
LE ROUDE 4
LEDOUX, A. 116
LEE, Branch W. 103 Thomas B. 33
LEECH, William 92
LEEDS, John 101
LEFEVRE, Mr. 23
LEMOYNE, F. A. 24
LEON, Francis 19
LEPPER, Mr. 31
LESLIE, John 7
LEVACHEZ, Virg. 68
LEVFEBRE, E. 33
LEVY, J. 24 S. L. 47
LEWIS, Hugh 93
LILE, William 53
LILLARD & Mosby 98
LOCKE, Samuel 15
LOCKETT, E. 104
LOCKHART, S. M. 17
LOCOUL 81
LOMBARD, Edward 102
LONGCOPE, C. S. 3
LUSK, L. Y. 79
LUZENBERG, Dr. 26
LYNCH, Charles 112
LYNN, Madame 9

MACKIE, Monroe 105
MAGUIRE, Francis 8
MAILET, J. B. 82

MALONE, Thomas C. 121
MARCHESSAU, A. 115
MARTE, Miguel 33
MARTEE, Mr. 22
MARTHESSEAU, Come 110
MARTIN, James H. 68 Mr. 125 Robert 77 Victor 90 William H. 93
MARTY, Mr. 25
MARVEL, A. D. 83
MASON, G. B. 49 80 115
MAXENT, J. B. P. 32
MAYO, Capt. 57 William 105
MCAULEY, Daniel 81
MCCANN, Daniel 35
MCCLEAN, John 88
MCCLINTOCK, T. R. 112
MCCLORY, Hugh 72
MCCLUSTER 24
MCFARLANE, Dr. 96
MCFARMER, Samuel 114
MCFREELY, Mr. 111
MCGEHEE, Abraham 2
MCGOVERN, J. 85
MCHUTTON, James A. 99
MCLAURIN, Daniel 63
MCLEGGAN, John 126
MCMULLEN, Catherine 108
MEADS, Mr. 29
MELANCON, Mrs. Joseph 85
MERRICK, George 6
MERRYFIELD, Mr. 56
METCALF, M. 113
MEUX, Thomas O. 74

MEYER, Charles 7 74
MIDDLETON, D. 65 David
    42 61
MIESEGAES, O. H. 89
MILLER, Henry W. 41 J. F.
    57 Mr. 106 William J. 55
MILLIGAN, Mr. 38
MILLS, Thomas 25
MINOR, W. J. 92
MINTURN, John 5
MIX, Mr. 72
MONTGOMERY, L. 109
MOORE, C. 113 Charles 108
    Henry 120 Henry E. 124
    Joseph H. 103
MORES, David 95
MORGAN, Col. Charles 21
    William H. 91
MORISON, H. N. 21
MORRES, D. 107
MORTEE, T. J. 79
MORTON, Mr. 29
MOSBY, J. F. 39
MOSES, Samuel L. 93
MOULLE, Mr. 13
MULLIKEN, Mr. 101
MURPHY, Daniel 51 James
    S. 121 Richard 35
MURRAY, Mrs. M. 116
    Nicholas 27
MUTTER, Ann 24
MYERS, H. C. 21

NADAUD, Mr. 41
NANSEN, Hiram 119
NEAL, John C. 12

NELSON, Mr. 22
NEWBERRY, John 105 116
NICAUD, Mr. 26 38
NICHOLS, Mr. 19 Nathan 13
    R. F. 62 72
NOBLE, J. R. 91
NORFLY, Mr. 20
NORMAN, Mr. 27
NORTH, Richard 53
NORTON, Mr. 27
NUTT, R. 92

OGDEN, R. N. 42
OSBURY, Capt. 20
OTWIG, Mr. 35
OXLEY, Charles 94
O'CALLAGHAN, Mr. 100
O'NEIL, Charles 54

PADON, Jesse 40
PAGE, Daniel D. 12 Mrs. 42
PALFREY, H. W. 122
PALMER, A. D. 65 75
PARK & Ryan 41
PARKER, Mr. 105 William
    68
PARKHURST, Cyrus 43
PARRA, F. Y. 100
PATTERSON, G. W. 102
PAYNE, John 24
PECK, H. P. 29 W. A. 65
PEHAU, Ulysee 51
PENCHON, Mr. 53
PERANA, Lewis 125
PERCH, Michelle 18
PERCY family 15

PERDEAUX, Silphide 68
PERKS, Mr. 18
PERRO, Mr. 30
PERRY, John G. 43
PESIGO, M. L. 102
PETERS, Samuel J. 65
PETERSON, H. F. 65 Mr. 98 105
PHILLIPS, Alex 108
PHILLIPS, Alexander 121
PHILLIPS, Bridget 48
PHILLIPS, Daniel 37
PHILLIPS, J. P. 123 James 38 67 70 78 80 124 R. 76
PICKETT, Nathaniel 115
PILCHER & Rayburn 62
PINCARD, Mr. 94
PIPKIN, Isaac 100 117 120
PIQUESNI, Dominic 125
PITTPAIN, Mr. 18
PLAUCHE, Adolphe 79
PLEASANCE, Francis 47
PLEMINGS, Thomas 80
POCHELU, Richard 77
POINCY, D. 106
POLK, W. 108 William 103
POPE, Britton J. 52
POPULUS, Celestine 80
PORTER, Dr. 96 Miss. 28 William 14
POWELL, B. W. 121 E. E. 120 Thomas 31
POWERS, James L. 117-118
PRAUCHE, Mr. 13
PREHN, William 77
PREHON, Alphonse 102

PRESTON, Mr. 37
PRICE, Elizabeth 110 Jim 13
PRIESTLY, James 61
PRIEUR, J. A. 100
PROCTOR, Col. 46 S. R. 97
PUCHEU, Madam 3
PUGH & Tucker 103
PUGH, Augustin 96 124

QUIN, Irvin 27

RABASSA, John 83-84
RACOSTE, Mr. 18
RAGESE, Joseph 63
RAHDERS, John H. 68
RAILEY, Jane 42
RAMSEY, Mathew 7
RANDOLPH, John H. 110 Mr. 3 77
RANSDALE, Mr. 16
RAPHALE, Mr. 37
RAY, T. 113
RAYMOND, Miss M. 121
RAYON, Mr. 115
REED, George 110 James 53
REGGIO, Adolph 86 101
REGGIO, Auguste 45-46
REGNIER, Mr. 98 100
REINE, A. 22 M. 22
REYNARD, P. 69
REYNOLDS, J. M. 126
RICHARDS, Mr. 31
RIPPETOE, Albert H. 119
RITCHIE, Charles 90
RIVIERE, P. 6
ROBELLE, Mr. 19

ROBELOT, A. 73
ROBERTS, Mary 42
ROBERTSON, J. M. 85
   Mary 42 William F. 118
ROBETAILE, M. 6
ROBINSON, A. Sidney 60
ROBLAIN, Mr. 18
RODES, John 102
RODGERS, Dana 107
RODRIQUE, J. B. 84
ROGERS, David John 28
   John David 56 Mr. 66-67
   W. N. 121
ROLAND, Mr. 19
ROSENDALE, Ann 75
ROTCHFORD, P. 65
ROUNTREE, Mr. 20
ROUSSEAU, Mr. 113
ROUSSEL, Baptiste 67
ROWLING, Mr. 122
RUTHERFORD, Col. 53 Mr. 65
RYMON, Amelia 115

SAMPSON, Mr. 48
SANDERS, D. B. 40
SANDS, Mrs. A. 101
SARPE, Mr. 5
SAULE, Mr. 24
SCHRODER, Henry 112
SCOTT, Thomas W. 79
   William 48
SEWELL, E. W. 56
SHALL, E. P. 86 95 103
   George P. 9 11 15 21 36
   Mrs. 112 114

SHAVALL, Major 55
SHAW, E. P. 71
SHAWL, Madam 119
SHEILS, P. 32-33 66
SHELBY, Aaron 126
SHEPHERD, Aune E. 94
SHRODER, Capt. 12
SHUIDS, Elihu 5
SIDDLE & Stewart 29
SIMON, E. 88
SITICOTON, William 30
SLARK, R. 78
SLATTER, Mr. 9 64 N. F. 104
SLOANE & Co. 4
SMITH, Edward 30 George W. 97 Ira 121 John Jr. 17 John S. 117-118 Mr. 19 30
SNOWDEN, C. F. 86
SOBY, Mr. 35
SOILLARD, Mr. 52
SOMMERS, F. 47
SORIA, Mr. 59
SOSTHEFFLE, Roman 111
SPARK, Daniel P. 80
SPEARING, Mary 45
SPROULE, Joseph A. 56
SQUIRES, George W. 44
ST. AMAN, O. O. 105
ST. PAUL, Henry 104
STAMP, William 29
STANSBURY, D. N. 54
STARK, D. W. 83 T. O. 82
STATLER, S. F. 41

STERLING, Mr. 30 R. G. 120
STERRETT, James R. 54
STEVENSON, John A. 49 66 87
STEWART, Col. 98 Mrs. S. 86 Samuel 102
STONE, Dr. 35 Mr. 31 Warren 63
STORUS, Mr. 28
STUART, J. A. 17 25
STUTSON, S. B. 55
SUGGIT, Thomas 8
SUMMERS, P. 22
SWENEY, George 118
SYLVESTER, James H. 3

TABONY, Mr. 44
TALBERT, Thomas L. 107
TANEY, C. H. 44
TANNY, C. H. 37
TAYLOR, George 40
TAYLOR, James M. 2 5 Mary S. 82 W. B. G. 14 52
TELLON, Peter 85
TERBONNE, Mr. 20
THOMPSON, James 55 Mr. 16 24 Sarah 22 William T. 94-95 101
THONKE, C. F. 31 48
TILGHMAN, T. O. 108
TIMMONEY, Mrs. 36
TODD, James D. 69
TORRES, Miguel 52
TOURNE, P. M. 4 87

TOWNSEND, I. D. 82
TRACY, E. L. 45 67 97 Mrs. 36
TRAVIS, Seaborn 112
TREGPAGNIER, Hippolyte 96
TREMOULET, Mr. 127
TRICOU, Mr. 66
TRIGAUT, Mr. 57
TRIMMELL, John 16
TUCKER, James A. 58
TURNELL, J. S. 25
TURNER, S. 96 Sewal T. 96 W. E. 33 78 92 111
TWITCHELL, T. C. 126
TYSON, James 64

UNRUH, John R. 7
UREE, Joseph 66
UZEE, Joseph 56

VALETTE, Antoine 25
VALMAUR, Mr. 27
VANCE, J. A. 89
VANDRELL, G. 45
VAUGHN, Samuel 94
VERDELET, Alex 88
VERMION, Valdice 53
VIGO, Joe 58
VILLARDE, Mr. 16
VILLIERE, Jules 90
VINER, John H. 22
VOORHES, M. T. 21

WADE, H. F. 1 2 11 34 46 75 95

WADSWORTH, T. M. 14 78
WALLACE, A. H. & Co. 10
WALSH, Mr. 19
WALTON, J. B. 60
WARNER, Dr. 15
WATSON, William 41
WEBB, Amos 33 William 125
WEEKS, P. J. 101
WEIL, H. 72
WELLS, George 27
WELSH, Mr. 7
WENDELL, Capt. 125
WHEELER, D. 112
WHITALL, Joseph E. 109
WHITE, Charles 67 J. R. 114 John 118 Judge 8 Martin 33 Maunsel 82 88 Sally 53
WHITEHEAD, William M. 14
WHITING, Mr. 29
WILKINS, Mr. 35
WILKINSON, Joseph B. 9 82 Mr. 37 N. N. 26 R. A. 8 82 Robert A. 123 W. W. 34
WILLIAMS, A. P. 47 Boyd 91 James 76 Mr. 39 T. 28 William H. 81
WILSON, A. G. 32 W. C. 102
WINGATE, David R. 76
WINSTON, T. B. 46 Thomas B. 15 25
WOLFE, T. 66 Thomas R. 79
WOODLAND, J. W. 74
WOODS, Mr. 58 William 48
WOODVILLE, Mr. 39
WOOLDRIDGE, A. D. 73
WOOLFOLK, Austin 94
WOOLFORT, Austin 22
WOOSTER, Madame 42
WRIGHT, James 40 L. B. 90

YANCEY, C. D. 109 E. L. 112
YORKE, Edward 53
YOUNGBLOOD, Thomas B. 83

ZUNTS, Mr. 111
ZUNTZ, James E. 85 Mr. 60

Index

Slaves, Full Name

ALEXANDER, Robert 115
ARMSTRONG, Henry 111

BAPTIST, John 56
BAPTISTE, John 124
BEE, William 46
BELL, John 6
BENNETT, Isaac 3
BRADLEY, George 46
    William 87
BREGIS, Oster 81
BRICE, John 86
BROWN, Isaac 98 Lucy 48
BULL, John 55, 106
BURNS, Henry 62

CAMPBELL, Sam 103
CARR, Jim 124
CLARKSON, Jim 51
COLLINS, Margaret 101
COOK, Edward 41
COOS, Jim 52
CORSEY, James 84
COYLE, John 62
CRAWFORD, Henry 97
CRISWELL, Mary 110
CUNNINGHAM, John 40

DAVIS, John 18
DODSON, Mary 77

DUGAS, John 57
DUNN, Oscar 50
DUSNAN, John 104
DYGS, John 86

EDWARDS, John 96

FOSTER, William 58
FRAZIER, Dick 106

GARDNER, Isaac 101
GILLMORE, Robert 27
GLOVER, Dave 103
GREEN, William 40
GRIFFIN, Dick 82
GUY, George 88

HARDY, John 62
HARRIS, Prince 19
HARRISON, John 78
HARVEY, Tom 55
HILL, Charles 126
HUNTER, John 75
INSKO, Abram 73

JACKSON, Henry 65
JOHNSON, Barnet 112
    Bennett 112 Hanna 114
    James 125 Star 122
JONES, Mary Ann 11

JORDAIN, Caroline 33
JOSEPH, John 115
JOSEY, Jim Along 69

KEER, John 98
KNIGHT, John 102

LAMAR, John 94
LEE, Ann 108
LEWIS, John 32
LOCKWOOD, Sarah 88

MACKEY, Henry 121
MALANE, Bob 114
MCMULLEN, Joe 108
MEDLEY, Madison 20
MISSOURI, Bill 120
MITCHELL, John 9
MONTEGUT, Robert 92
NELSON, John 87

PASSAGUAY, Felix 63
PENN, James 108
PERKINS, Arthur 61
PERRY, John 36
PETERSON, Alex 51
PHILIP, Louis 85
PHILIPS, Thomas 26
PHILLIPS, Henry 96
PIERRE, Jack 13
PRICE, Jim 13 William 42

RANDOLPH, John 110
RICH, John 39

RICHARDSON, James 8
ROBERTSON, James 78

SHIRLEY, Tom 10
SIPP, Henry 120
SMART, John 55
SMITH, Ebenezer 100
    Ferdinand 39 George 99
    113 Stephen 125
SOLET, John 9
SPEARS, Harrison 45
SPINK, William 121
SYPHAX, George 46

TAYLOR, David 103 Henry
    107 John 78 Sam 117
    Thomas 15, 25
TEAMS, Jesse 106
THOMAS, Ephemy 116
TOUSAINT, Harriet 6
TRIPPLET, Herbert 14
TURNER, Nelson 103

WALLACE, William 78, 92,
    111
WASHINGTON, William
    107
WHITE, George 93 John 117
    MARIA 99
WILLIAM, Grand 63
WILLIAMS, Hannibal 57
    POMPEY 104
WILSON, Henry 80, 97 Jo 27
    JOHN 9

WONSLY, Tom 103

Index

Slaves, First Name Only

Aaron 16 24 34
Abby 96
Aberdeen 7
Abraham 35 45 93
Abram 49 73 121
Adaline 113
Adam 12 17 31
Addison 80
Aga 24
Aggy 6 43
Agnes 68
Albert 54 58 104 110
Aleck 81
Alex 37
Alexander 104
Alford 47
Alfred 20 45 50 75 104
Allen 21
Alpheus 55
Amanda 119
Amee 93
Amelia 19 28 38
Amos 111
Amy 10
Anderson 10 14 20 35 81
Andrew 5 18 23 51 78 123
Ann 16 49 66 87
Anna 91
Annette 78
Anthony 59 61

Apollo 18
Archey 20
Archy 56
Ary 14
Asiner 31
Auguste 53 65
Augustus 19
Austin 94

Baptiste 46 108
Barbara 64
Bartlett 79
Ben 16 80 86 119 121
Benjamin 110
Bennett 112
Beny 12
Berry 57 64
Betsey 18 50
Betsy 30 59 63 72 105 116
Beverly 50
Big Dick 76
Bill 9 15 26 31 58 62 76 81
   91 101 106 122 126
Billy 64
Bob 7 27-28 30 87 98 108
   117
Bogs 75
Booker 21
Bos 74
Boston 90

Bouka 85
Brazile 124
Brown 104 114
Burrel 16 74
Byron 122

Caesar 11 79 125
Caleb 16
Calloway 120
Calviz 10
Camden 94
Caroline 2 27 60 64
Carter 66
Cary 85
Casimer 31
Cassey 69
Cassimer 76
Catherine 7-8 37 49 69
Celeste 53 62 113
Celestin 97
Celia 1 113
Chance 127
Chapeau 38
Charles 11 18 27 30 35 46 51
    73 75 86 92-93 106 115
    122
Charlotte 15 26 57 73 77 95
    116
Cherinettea 51
Christine 118
Claiborne 29
Clara 64
Clarissa 7
Clem 103
Clemire 67
Clinton 70 89

Colbert 8
Colin 84
Cora 100
Corinne 60
Cornelius 42 47 60
Cressy 124
Cresy 40
Cudjoe 86
Cupid 125
Cyrus 58

Dalger 46 54
Dan 38 45 80
Daniel 26 50 90 97
Dapne 50
Dave 14 59 80 89
David 18 21 31 53 84 89 101
Davis 101
Delia 34
Delphi 67
Delphie 63
Denis 120
Dennis 12 112
Diana 21 49 66
Dick 124
Dick 4 34 39 79 97 124
Dido 2
Diego 56
Dorsey 2

Ebon 49
Edey 111
Edmond 10 79 87 112 123
Edmund 22 40 59 62 70
Edward 28 96 109 119
Elba 114

Eli 126
Elijah 123
Eliza 3 19 22 44 46 52 56
    59-60 71 73-74 76 85 94
Elizabeth 5 19 26 31 44
Ellen 10 90
Ellick 17 29 78 104
Ellis 32-33 66
Emanuel 105
Emelia 82
Emeline 54
Emerson 67 97
Emiline 78
Emille 67
Emma 51 78
Enoch 45
Ephraim 34 39
Ephram 39
Esther 83
Eugenia 113
Evelina 12

Fanny 35 67 77 96
Felicianna 97
Felix 63
Feme 116
Festus 118
Fevrier 83
Field 10 39
Foster 78
Fountain 61 65 111
Frances 11
Francis 24 32 35
Francois 38
Frank 18 54 106 113 117-118
Frederick 26 102

French 9 92
Frontin 78
Garrison 35
General 65
George 3-6 10 12 19 25 29 41
    48 56 67 77 80 107-110
    113-115
Gilbert 94
Godfrey 82
Grand William 63
Granville 32
Green 29
Griffin 35 75
Grundy 108
Gustave 24

Hal 60
Hamilton 37 90
Hamlet 90
Hana 108
Hannah 1 28 62 76 88 114
Hardy 53
Harriet 66 89 118
Harriet Jane 72
Harriett 42 58 76
Harris 34
Harrison 34 70 103
Harry 18 29 65 83 118 124
Hector 30
Henderson 92
Henri 110
Henry 4 14 16 19 25 28 35 37
    38-39 57 59 64-65 83 88
    102-103 109 116 118
    121 124-125
Hercules 125

Hetty 99
Hilaye 26
Hiram 94
Horace 64
Hubbard 32 86
Humphrey 72

Ike 50
Iris 49
Irvin 115
Isaac 16 23 43 50 63 86 91
    111 121
Isak 72
Isam 72 113
Isom 111 126

J. C. 97
Jack 4 9 17 38 42 53 58 65 80
    83 87 90 95 116 119
Jackson 3 46
Jacob 18 22 84 100 127
Jacques 101
Jago 23
Jake 23
James 12 20 47
Jane 15 45 72 83 98 125
Janet 103
January 11 61
Jarrett 22
Jean 80
Jeffer 116
Jefferson 27
Jenny 6
Jerry 34 100 116 126

Jim 4 14 18-19 23 34 48 49
    54 56 63 70-71 81 84 86
    91-92 94-95 108
Jim Along Josey 69
Job 27 91
Joe 18-19 77 97-98 105-106
    108 122
John 5 8 16 19 20 31 33
    35-37 52 55 57 68 70 78
    81 83 85 103 105
    110-111 119 125
Johnson 122
Jordan 59
Judy 37 81 102
Julia 37 102
Julianne 37

Kesiah 30
Kincaid 92
King 99
Kit 98
Kitty 20 56

Lee 69
Leek 48
Leonard 30 36
Leroy 2
Let 41
Lettitia 41
Lettus 12
Letty 68
Levi 17 123
Lewis 17 26 40 103 112
    119-120
Liddy 104
Litty 90

Liz 12
Liza 107
London 66
Lorenzo 10
Loucinda 8
Louicene 24
Louis 26 33 67 106
Louisa 18-19 46 48 54 77 95 99 107 118
Louise 7 65 101
Louisianne 24
Lucien 89
Lucinda 16 65
Lucy 28 32 52 74
Luke 45-46
Lydia 104

Mace 2 29
March 111
Margaret 25 106
Marguerite 38
Maria 7 16 22 32 35 58-59 66
Mariah 1-2 59
Marie 44
Martha 35 41 75 102 116
Mary 21 28 30-31 35 44-45 50 55 77 90 116
Mary Ann 5 14 36 47 58 74-75 100-101
Mary Anne 27 87
Mary Ellen 109
Mary Jane 9 111
Mason 29 40
Mathy 90
Matilda 43 96 102
May 127

Meranthe 66
Mike 109 112
Miles 99
Millie 24
Milly 42 117
Mima 75
Minerva 53
Mingo 121
Minor 45 116
Miyadline 123
Montgomery 103
Morgiana 91
Morna 71
Morris 95 103
Mose 96
Moses 32 43 53 60 66-67 96 116 120

Name 84
Nan 5
Nancy 8 22 31 48 59 68-70 72 84 91 97
Nannah 5
Narry 84
Nat 18
Nathan 5 20
Ned 6 13-14 38 49 70 82 103 109-110
Needham 68
Nelson 13 17-18 71 79 107 120
Newton 10
Niase 49
Norvell 42

Oscar 100

Pamella 126
Patrick 10 44
Paul 122
Pauline 26
Payton 28
Pelagie 40
Pete 95
Peter 4 22-23 25 28 38 41 55
    57 71 74 76 79 89
    105-107 122 126
Peterson 34
Phere 52
Phil 70 89 94
Philander 89
Philip 38-39 70 116
Phill 78
Phillis 54
Pierre 40
Pitt 106
Pleasant 110
Polly 26 110
Pricilla 23
Primas 60
Primus 11 30 48
Prince 113
Prissa 31

Queen 88

Rachal 104
Rachel 71 90
Ralph 12
Randle 39
Randolph 24
Raphael 44 46

Reason 3
Rebecca 19 23 25 75
Reuben 65
Richard 70 76 113
Ripley 17
Robert 15 20 25 46 50 74 85
    92 109
Romaine 120
Rosa 2
Rosana 92
Rosanna 68
Rose 20
Rosine 57
Roxana 70
Ruben 30 116
Rufus 10

Sabrina 3
Saintville 24
Sally 18 22 30 66 82 91
Sam 8 13 20-21 25 28 38 52
    65 69 79 81 89 98 109
    112 120
Sampson 14
Sana 119
Sandy 37 95 124
Sarah 15 20 28-30 53 82 91
    93 109 111 114 122
Sarah Ann 33 74
Scot 20
Scye 45
Sidney 8 10 25 81
Simon 64 83 85 117-118
Simpson 16
Sims 64
Sinus 63

Solomon 13 32 41 91
Sophy 115
Squire 56
St. Jean 126
Stephen 7 58 64 102 125
Sterling 53
Stuttering Bill 58
Sukey 13
Susan 10 12 13 83 117

Thisby 115
Thomas 61
Thornton 111
Toby 37 119
Tom 9 23 26 43 53 56 60 87
    93 98 106 112 116
Toney 61 93
Tony 93 121
Turner 4

Vardeman 65
Venice 37
Venus 94

Victoire 19
Victor 69
Victoria 75 85
Vina 27
Vincent 101
Violet 5
Virgile 120
Walker 63
Wallace 44 92
Washington 6 8 55 73 116
    123
Westley 27 42
Wiley 83 108 114
Will 33
William 3 9 11 16 18 27-30
    33-34 38 41 43 47 60-61
    63 69 79 86 88 91-92 96
    98-101 110-111 115 126
Wilson 57 59 73 101
Winny 85
Worner 3
Wright 50

Zephir 18

www.ingramcontent.com/pod-product-compliance
Lightning Source LLC
Chambersburg PA
CBHW071609170426
43196CB00034B/2247